Also by Sandy Kraemer

Books and Select Professional Publications

60-Minute Estate Planner (three editions plus CD and software)
Solar Law, Present and Future (plus 21 annual supplements)
Connecting People of All Ages
Inheriting America
Inheritance and Human Rights
Inheritance Protects Human Rights

Games

15 new commercial games and recreational/sport equipment items (with patents) licensed to national companies including 3M, Parker Brothers, Cadaco, Pacific Games, and Park & Sun Sports.

More Reader Comments

"Kraemer's new paradigm provides explicit guidance that diplomats, and everyone else, should use in negotiations."
— Gerald Scott, United States ambassador to United Nations

"Asking requires making choices. People of all ages should read Sandy Kraemer's book to become higher achievers."
—Arnold R. Weber, president emeritus, Northwestern University

"ASK is a must-read for high achievers."
—Bill Hybl, CEO, El Pomar Foundation; past president, United States Olympic Committee

This little book is more valuable than gold."
—Marvin Strait, past chairman, American Institute of Certified Public Accountants

"Every lawyer who follows the concepts in this book will become a better advocate. Every client who reads this book will be more successful."
— Larry R. Gaddis, attorney, bar association president

"Valuable life stories read like a good novel."
—Robert Knapp, Ph.D., economist

"Sandy Kraemer's message gives everyone permission to ask."
— Colleen Baldrica, school counselor and author

"ASK has encouraged me to be less shy about asking for help. The positive generous responses have been surprising."
—Jim Flynn, newspaper columnist

"*HOW TO ASK* puts the biblical directive—ask, search, find—into action."
—The Rev. Dr. Paul R. Peel, senior pastor

"Everyone who has read the bestseller *The 7 Habits of Highly Effective People* by Stephen Covey should read *HOW TO ASK* by Sandy Kraemer."
—Phil Winslow, CEO and owner of large new car dealerships

"Every entrepreneur and non-profit fundraiser should read *HOW TO ASK*. I am giving copies to business associates and fundraisers in a YMCA capital campaign."
—Keith Ketelsen, businessman and charity volunteer

"Empowering! I will give copies of the *ASK* book to family and friends."
—Lena Gail Case, teacher, wife, mother and grandmother

"A survival handbook for college students. If you don't ask for help, you won't get it."
—Autumn Kruis, university student

HOW TO ASK
The 5 Win Words

Sandy Kraemer

Fourth Edition

East of the Mountains  and West of the Sun

RHYOLITE PRESS LLC
Colorado Springs, Colorado

Copyright © 2020, Sandy Kraemer

All Rights Reserved. No portion of this book may be reproduced in any form or by any electronic or mechanical means, including information storage and retrieval systems, without permission from the publisher, except by a reviewer who may quote brief passages in a review.

Published in the United States of America by Rhyolite Press LLC
P.O. Box 60144
Colorado Springs, Colorado 80960
www.rhyolitepress.com

Kraemer, Sandy

How To Ask

First edition published 2013. Fourth edition March 1, 2020.

Library of Congress Control Number: 2020932510
ISBN 978-1-943829-13-2

Publisher's Cataloging-in-Publication Data

Names: Kraemer, Sandy Frederick, 1937-, author.
Title: How to ask : the 5 win words , fourth edition / Sandy Kraemer.
Description: Colorado Springs, CO: Rhyolite Press, LLC, 2020.
Identifiers: LCCN 2020932510 | ISBN 9781943829132
Subjects: LCSH Patient advocacy. | Self-care, Health. | Health literacy. | Patient education. | Physician and patient. | Medical personnel and patient.| Communication in medicine. | Assertiveness (Psychology) | Patient-centered health care. | BISAC MEDICAL / Physician & Patient | SELF-HELP /Communication & Social Skills.
Classification: LCC R118 .K728 2020 | DDC 610.696 --dc23

PRINTED IN THE UNITED STATES OF AMERICA

Cover design, book design/layout by Donald R. Kallaus

This Fourth Edition is dedicated to all those who need help, with a bonus focus on asking for medical care.

CONTENTS

Introduction   xi

Part I: The Five Win Words

Asking for Medical Care Bonus!	1
Rags to Riches	15
PERSISTENCE	21
SINCERITY	29
HUMILITY	37
HONESTY	45
BELIEF	55

Part II: Ask for Wants

Plan to Ask	69
Ask for Money	75
Ask for Love	81
Ask for Opportunity	87
Ask for Jobs	91
Ask for Heath	97
Ask for Justice	101
List Your Wants	107
Spotlight Your Wants	111
The Circle of Wants	117
Circles of People	119

Part III: Priceless Insights

Get Insights	131
Commonplacing	133
Wit with Wisdom	137
Bottom Uppers and Top Downers	147
Be Vulnerable	153
The Law of One	157
Tell a Story	161
Managing Askers	165
Five-Star Askers	169
The Win-Win Outcome	175

Appendix 179

Your *ASK EFFECTIVELY* Action Plan	181
Your *ASK EFFECTIVELY* Rating	183
Humble Thanks	185

INTRODUCTION

Fourth edition includes more about medical care because readers have asked for more help. Applying the *5 Win Words* to ask effectively for medical care saved my life.

We all have unfulfilled wants. Are any of these on your short list?

- Negotiate a better price
- Receive timely healthcare
- Have an uncommon experience
- Build an organization
- Develop new friendships
- Earn more money
- Raise money for a charity
- Secure a better job
- Find a good partner
- Enjoy better sex
- Resolve a dispute
- Lead a group
- Reduce debts
- Pay less in taxes

- Plea bargain a traffic ticket
- Gain more education and training

In my professional career as a counselor-at-law, I have worked with more than 5,000 people who have asked for my help to achieve personal goals. Some had already experienced incredible success in getting what they wanted; others, disastrous failure. Many had simply received far less than they had hoped for. But whatever their outcome, they all had one thing in common: Each came to me with a story to tell.

As a councelor, it was my job to listen and assist them in reaching their goals in whatever way I could. And frankly, that was my stroke of good fortune. Listening gave me an opportunity to learn.

My clients became my teachers, and the lessons they offered have been humbling. I've learned more from them than I could from an entire library of self-help books. In the pages that follow, I hope to share this knowledge with you.

My most successful rags-to-riches client, referred to as "Big R" throughout this book, claims that asking for help is the very basis of his success. Together, we have identified "5 Win Words" essential to effective asking. By applying them, you can quickly turn wants into realities.

These Win Words describe habits of reasoning necessary to ask effectively. They identify a pattern of thought that consistently produces the best outcomes. I discovered this new paradigm by professionally observing over 5,000 people seeking to fulfill their needs and desires—their wants.

HOW TO ASK calls for unconventional thinking. It is not written exclusively for linear readers who always turn from page to consecutive page. Rather, it offers the freedom to pick a subject of special interest, a life story, or a random section. You will find important observations and telling quotations throughout. Graphics illustrate the concepts, encouraging you to think beyond any self-limiting boundaries.

As you come upon items that are of particular interest, or that spur new thoughts or ideas, please consider writing in the margins or dog-earing pages. At points in the book, there are exercises that invite you to write in your answers; go for it. Use it as a workbook. Do whatever will help you make the most out of reading this book.

I hope you'll discover, as I did, that by observing the actions and reactions of the people around you, insights become launching pads to higher levels of personal fulfillment. You will receive help by asking effectively.

Part I

The 5 Win Words

Including . . .

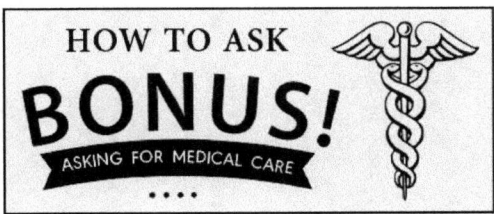

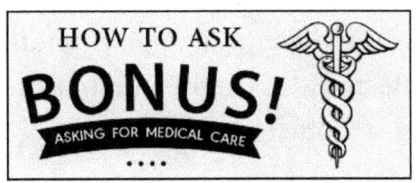

ASKING FOR MEDICAL CARE

At 9:30 p.m., sitting at my desk at home, I knew I was suffering from life threatening congestive heart failure. I picked up my ASK book and reread Milton Waldron M.D. surgeon's prophetic quote, "Sandy Kraemer's ASK book will save lives. Good health depends on knowing how to ask for help." I realized his call to action applied to me that night. I needed immediate medical care from the best possible provider. I logged on to my computer and started typing. The rest of the story follows titled "An E-Mail Saved My Life."

Many readers of How to Ask volunteer their personal patient and advocacy stories of life changing experiences asking for medical care. Outcomes, both good and bad, often include heart felt opinions of how they would do it differently if there is a next time. "I did not know where to go?" "Who to ask?" "What to ask?" "Who are the best doctors?" "The best hospitals?" "The right treatment?" "Medications?"

The good news is that from my personal life changing events and the medical care experiences of others, the five Win Words paradigm clearly applies to asking effectively for medical care. The Win Words are: Persistence, Sincerity, Humility, Honesty and Belief.

More medical care stories and insights are added to *How to Ask–Fourth Edition,* as an introductory bonus, rather than integrated into the *Ask for Health* section beginning at page 97, because there is a medical emergency. The health care industry is at political, professional, technological and financial tipping points. Both patients and providers must effectively ask more questions to make the tipping points opportunities for better medical care.

Patients and Providers

Everyone as a patient or patient advocate will need to ask for life changing medical care at some time. Doctors, nurses, physician assistants, medical assistants and administrators as medical care providers will need to make accurate diagnosis and deliver effective and timely treatments. Do you know the most effective questions to ask? As a patient, advocate or provider, are you ready? Will you timely ask the correct questions? Will the answers be correct and understood? Will the results be the best outcome?

I asked health care patient and providers the same question: "How do people ask for health care?"

Patients answered: "It's a Provider monopoly." "Patients think doctors are God and should not be questioned." "Be an advocate and ask someone to help advocate for you." "Ask others about their experiences." "Have a plan." "Ask for favors." "Stay engaged." "Be willing to change." "Trust the system." "Pray a lot."

Providers answered: "It is a horrible problem." "A huge challenge." "Patients don't answer questions accurately." "Patients understate their illness." "Blame providers for treatment failure." "Need measurable criteria for judging providers."

Health care providers and suppliers have created legal shields to protect against liability claims. These shields make effectively asking for medical help even more challenging.

Stories motivate. Information informs. With the speed and volume of new information, life-changing stories remain highly memorable. Let me begin with my own.

An E-Mail Saved My Life

My congestive heart failure was progressing quickly with shortness of breath, pain down my back, frightening fluid retention and no sleep. My new cardiologist was the third treating physician I had consulted still looking for the best outcome. He was the first to recommend a Trans-Catheter Aortic Valve Replacement (TAVR) instead of open-heart surgery to replace the failing heart valve I had previously replaced thirteen years ago. Also, the first two treating physicians did not consider urgency.

On Tuesday, April 2 at 9:36 p.m., I sent an e-mail to the address listed on the professional card of my new cardiologist stating: "…time is of essence. Is there any possibility you would be available this week to perform the surgery?" He e-mailed me back at 10:14 p.m. stating: "I will investigate. Usually not possible to get team together on days other than Wednesday. A nurse will be calling."

The nurse called late Thursday to advise that the team would be available Friday morning with surgery scheduled for 8:30 a.m. When I was wheeled into surgery, I counted ten waiting team members. The procedures took 90 minutes. I was discharged on Saturday afternoon and walked one and a half miles on Monday!

The cardiologist later told me on a scale of 1-4, with 4 being the worst heart condition, mine was a 4+ with over 60% blood regurgitation. If I believed in miracles, this experience would qualify.

I gave the cardiologist a copy of my book *HOW TO ASK*. I had applied the Win Words to effectively ask for health care. Days later he e-mailed: "I am reading the book you gave me. Thank you. I focused on the humility chapter since it is my father's birthday today. He died five years ago and taught me, by example, humility. You are amazing!" In fact, the cardiologist, not me, is amazing, and humble.

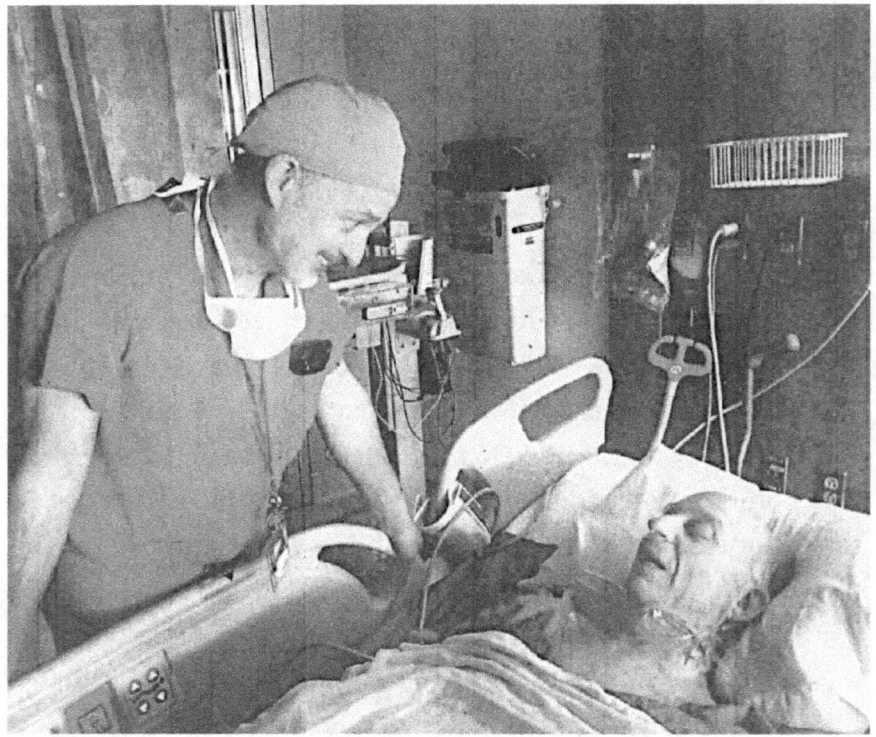

John Carroll, M.D., treating cardiologist, with Sandy Kraemer, patient, in recovery room after successful emergency Trans-Catheter Aortic Valve Replacement (TAVR). Photograph by Christina Dinegar, daughter of patient.

Why me?

Katherine, a forty-seven-year-old wife and mother of three, is a cancer survivor, although she has lived with cancer most of her adult life. Her medical files are filled with reports and notes from regular visits to the oncologist. She endured x-rays, ultrasounds, biopsies, surgeries, breast reconstruction, implants, chemotherapy, radiation, tamoxifen, blood tests and more. She reads the latest findings on new and promising drugs and vaccines.

Katherine relates, "Why me? I have asked that question more times than I care to count."

"The only answer I have that makes any sense is, it builds inner strength!" Somehow when faced with unexpected challenges, strengths pay a visit. The will to win becomes central. The challenges of managing to win sharpen the senses, expands circles of friends and medical providers.

"Family and friends have told me they could never go through what I have gone through. This statement is a curious one. I want to ask, 'Would the alternative be better?'"

"There is never a right time for anything in life. There is just a time. It has been my time to have breast cancer. I think of other people I know who have experienced far worse medical challenges. I don't feel sorry for them, I cheer them on."

"People ask, 'Are you angry, frustrated, depressed or sad?' My answer is always no, life plays out differently for everyone. I have been blessed, fortunate, happy, satisfied to have my life. I would not trade places with anyone."

Communication Failures

Patient and provider are most often strangers that have never met and may never meet again. They must build a temporary connecting bridge over which life changing communication may flow. The communications must be open, thoughtful, clear and correct. Two specific provider communication failures immediately come into focus.

When I was sixteen years old, I was told I had a heart mummer. This heart condition never slowed my running, mountain climbing or skiing. Thirteen years ago, I had open heart surgery to replace my congenitally defective aortic valve with a bioprosthetic valve made from the sac surrounding the heart of a cow. I was also diagnosed with an ascending aortic aneurism which was stable. I was told the bioprosthetic valve would last an average of seventeen years and I would have warning symptoms many months ahead of valve failure, allowing time for another valve replacement.

I always have an annual physical and see our family doctor three to four times a year for medical issues. Before leaving the office after every visit, I receive a computer-generated medical report which includes my medical history, medical problems, medications and recommended treatment. The physician creates these reports during the office visit by looking at his computer and typing while we talk. Several times I asked him to stop typing while we talk. He would then pick up a small sticky note pad and take notes for one or two minutes, then start typing again. The report from a twenty-minute routine visit averaged six pages. I quit reading the reports several years ago.

After my emergency lifesaving heart valve replacement described in the prior story, An E-Mail Saved My Life, I read some of my past computer-generated medical reports. Several listed under the Problems Section, "Congestive Heart Failure Onset 6/22/2018" more than seven months before my emergency valve replacement.

I confronted our family doctor and asked, "Why didn't you tell me, why didn't we talk about it?" Very softly he commented, "Oh, I'm sorry."

My first cardiologist evaluated my congestive heart failure symptoms and recommended another open-heart surgery, replacement of the aortic stem with the aneurism, and a local surgeon. The surgeon was on vacation and the staff could not schedule the surgery.

I sought a second opinion from another cardiologist. He recommended a non-invasive TAVR procedure and not to replace the still stable aneurism. When I told my first cardiologist that I had decided to go with the second cardiologist's recommendation, he responded, "I've been thinking about it. That's a good decision." The first cardiologist never mentioned the TAVR alternative to open heart surgery. Both patient, and provider, must keep asking questions, listening and responding until the best diagnosis and treatment becomes apparent.

A Special Favor

Debra became highly concerned as she watched Kevin, her husband of 32 years, become increasingly short of breath when he climbed a flight of stairs. At the top of the stairs he would hold the banister until his heavy breathing subsided. He stopped exercising at the health club, but continued to pay the monthly fee. When shopping together he did not drive and suggested finding a parking space close to the store. Kevin and Debra's evening walk and talk were a thing of the past.

Kevin went through a battery of tests regarding his heart health. The reports came back showing no abnormal condition. The cardiologist evaluation was completed with no recommended treatment. Kevin decided to do nothing. He speculated it must be a new seasonal allergy that would soon pass.

Debra persisted. She was told their health insurance would not pay for more tests. She did not know any provider. She talked to a friend who had family ties to a chief hospital administrator at the local hospital. Debra asked her friend for a special favor. Would she connect her directly to the chief administrator? Her friend did.

The administrator decided more tests may benefit and scheduled tests that might identify a condition covered by their health insurance. Kevin was scheduled to meet with a physician's assistant (PA). Consequently, more tests showed Kevin had a lung disease. With this diagnosis insurance coverage was provided and treatments were scheduled.

Debra sent an e-mail saying she had read my *How To Ask* book which motivated and guided her. She wrote, "I had never asked for a special favor like this before but my husband is my main priority. I persisted and my humility and sincerity kicked in."

Fourth Medical Opinion

Seven years after our marriage, with three children under six years old, my wife, Dorothy, started seeing a black spot peripherally in her left eye. She described it as appearing like a housefly that she could not swat away. It became a constant irritant that interfered with her vision. Eye drops did not help.

We sought a medical opinion from a friend who was a doctor specializing in ophthalmology. He could not diagnose the condition and referred us to a leading specialist in Denver. He also declined to make a diagnosis or recommend treatment. The condition began to worsen, a shadow appearing around the spot.

We continued to search for a diagnosis and a cure. We next turned to our trusted family doctor. He placed Dorothy in the hospital for three days of tests. Still with no conclusion, he referred us to a local ophthalmologist with a national reputation for treating uncommon eye diseases.

We scheduled an appointment, and I will never forget it. We told him of our frustration with having no diagnosis after examinations by three physicians. He listened and performed his own examination. Afterwards, he stated with confidence, "Dorothy has advanced *pars planitis*, a rare autoimmune disease of the pars plana, between the colored area of the eye and the choroid. She may lose the sight of her eye if untreated. I believe I can treat and effectively cure the eye. Treatment will include two very painful shots behind the eyeball."

Quickly, Dorothy and I agreed to proceed with treatment. The shots were painful and caused temporary debilitation. She left the outpatient procedure in a wheelchair. Before long, the cure was complete. Dorothy enjoys full eyesight. Persistence paid off. The fourth medical expert we consulted was the first one with the correct diagnosis and treatment plan.

Beware of the Back-Pain Industry

The majority of people experience back pain sometime in life. The pain may come and go intermittently causing mild discomfort, or become excruciatingly debilitating as it radiates down one or both arms or legs. Treating back-pain is a huge and growing industry including medical doctors, osteopathic doctors, chiropractors, physical therapist, nurses, physicians' assistants, hospitals, wellness clinics, prescriptions and non-prescription drugs, supplements, and therapeutic products. Back pain is a treatable but often incurable medical problem.

When friend Rick, who had read my ASK book, learned I was writing a new edition with a medical care focus, he volunteered his own story:

"My dad was a trim high school base ball player, considered an offer to play professionally, choose the university track, dropped out after two years, eloped and settled into a sedentary office job. He had two sons, Don and me. Dad's weight ballooned from 175 to 240. He spent summer evenings in a backyard hammock, listening to Cub's baseball games. He constantly complained of lower back pain. Said he had a congenitally deformed lumbar spine. He took pain and sleep medications, had epidural shots that temporarily reduced the pain and eventually had three back surgeries. He became weak, depressed and never stopped complaining about back pain until his death."

"By comparing x-rays, MRI's and CT Scans, my brother Don and I realized we had the same lumbar genetic deformities as Dad. Don has gone through the same lifestyle and medical experiences as Dad, weight gain and medications, epidural shots and three surgeries. He has a hard time walking fifty yards."

"The good news is I have avoided surgeries, am pain free and walk two to three miles a day. I think the way people manage back pain makes a huge difference. I weigh less than I did in high school, exercise regularly and learned from a physical therapist what physical work and exercises to avoid. When I have back pain, I limit my medications. The pain doctor said there were six spots in my lumbar spine where epidurals might reduce pain. I tried one, which helped temporarily, but have declined additional shots. I sleep on my back. I have learned how to manage back problems by always asking about recommended medical care choices and consistently choosing less treatment."

Who Will Ask For You?

What do you do when you can't advocate for yourself? What do you do when you can't ask others for help or for information that helps you make an important decision? Leonard tells his own life saving story.

"Ten years ago, I was at the airport getting ready to board a plane for a business trip. But waiting to go through airport security that day, I collapsed. They called it Sudden Cardiac Death. I didn't know it then, but there was only a 5% survival rate, and half of those surviving have brain damage. If a victim doesn't receive help in the first few minutes, there is no survival."

"After receiving CPR from a bystander, the paramedics arrived to use the defibrillator paddles to resuscitate me. I was brought by ambulance to the hospital where I stayed for nine days, most of that time in the cardiac ICU, and the first one to two critical days in a coma."

"What decisions had to be made regarding my health and who would make them for me? Who would be my advocate and who would fight for me if needed? Thankfully, I had my wife."

"A critical decision that needed to be answered right away was, 'Who would perform the needed surgery to implant a defibrillator in my chest to prevent this from happening again?'"

"The electrophysiologist who was on call strongly recommended that she perform the surgery right away. My wife stood up as my advocate and asked the surgeon, who was the best electrophysiologist to perform the surgery and what are the options for the medical device to insert. The doctor was not offended and told her, 'If it was me having the surgery, I would have Dr. Sauer do it. He's the best and he can recommend the best model device.'"

"Dr. Sauer performed the surgery to insert the device he recommended that later saved my life twice. He then performed another surgery that thankfully ended my having additional episodes of sudden cardiac death."

"In my case, having an advocate who asked the right questions and made the right decisions based on the information she received paid off for me in a big way. Many of us, including myself, don't question the "experts" and often settle for what others tell us we should do. It takes someone who is strong and confident to ask for what they want and to advocate for someone they care for, rather than just accept what they're told. It can make all the difference in the world."

Questions to Ask Your Medical Provider

- Tell me what you know about my medical problem?
- If there are test results pending, when and how will I receive the results?
- What's my treatment plan?
- What steps do I need to take and when?
- Why is the treatment you are proposing the best for me?
- What are alternative treatments?
- Who can you recommend for a second opinion?
- If a surgery or procedure is involved, how many of these have you performed?
- What will be my recovery period?
- What will be the follow-up treatment?
- How will this change my life?

Quotes

"A good physician treats the disease; the great physician treats the patient who has the disease."
—Sir William Osler, Canadian, Physician and founder of Johns Hopkins Hospital

"It may seem a strange principle to enunciate as the very first requirement in a hospital that it should do the sick no harm."
—Florence Nightingale, English social reformer and founder of modern nursing

"Often the best medicine is no medication at all, or the intervention is no intervention at all. But those conversations with patients that take the time to explain that the evidence simply does not support

doing a test or prescribing a drug are long conversations, and its much easier in clinical practice to order a test."
—Robyn Ward, Chair, Medical Services Advisory Committee, Commonwealth of Australia

"When a lot of remedies are suggested for a disease, that means it can not be cured."
—Anton Chekhov, Russian playwright and short-story writer

"He began to question and listen, and observe, and then to think differently about Anne's case. And by doing so, he saved her life, because for fifteen years a key aspect of her illness had been missed."
— Jerome Groopman, M.D., , Professor, Harvard Medical School, in *How Doctors Think* (Houghton Mifflin Co. 2007)

"True professionals provide considered advice. And sometimes doing nothing is exactly the right thing to do. The same is true for medicine. Recognize that the doctor who advises no action may be the one who really cured you."
— Dr. Gilbert H. Welch, Physician and cancer researcher

"Always laugh when you can. It is cheap medicine."
— Lord Byron, English poet and politician

"Beware of surgeons with big mortgages."
—Milton Waldron, M.D., Surgeon

"The physician, who, having just forbidden his cardiac patient indulgence in tobacco, alcohol and amorous intimacies, was asked by the victim, 'Tell me doctor, if I give these up, will I live longer?' to which his physician replied with charm and candor, 'No it will only seem longer.'"
—Bernard Meyer, Ph.D., author of dispute resolution books

RAGS TO RICHES

While driving to a football game, I asked Big R, my friend and most successful rags-to-riches client, what he wanted to do with the rest of his life. At first, his reply made me laugh out loud. Then it gave me pause—because the more I thought about it, the more clearly I understood that his answer was like a floodlight illuminating a hidden pathway in the dark.

In that brief, memorable conversation, he revealed the secret of his life's ever-flowing abundance:

"I want to teach people how to beg," he reflected, with an uncommonly serious tone in his voice.

"Why?" I inquired with a smile.

"All my life, I've gotten what I wanted by applying one simple strategy—I beg people for help. It might be rewarding to teach others to do the same."

That's when I laughed. "Seems a little simplistic. You want to build a second career teaching people to beg?"

"I guess it does sound simple when you say it out loud. The word 'beg' may overstate what I'm trying to say. 'Ask' is a more accurate word than beg. And it's not really simple. You can't just ask. You have to know who to ask and how to ask that person effectively."

Now the idea was beginning to intrigue me. "So you're telling me you'd like to teach people how to ask effectively?"

"Yes," Big R replied, his voice resounding with confidence.

"Are there certain words or phrases you have to use to ask effectively?"

He tilted his head in thought as we sped down the highway. "Maybe not use particular words when you're asking. It's more like keeping certain words in mind, applying certain words to guide your approach."

"Like what words?" I quizzed, with growing interest.

"Well, let me think. Persistence, humility ... there must be more words that encourage positive bottom-line outcomes. Words that create a win-win situation for everyone involved."

"Win Words?" I spontaneously exclaimed.

"Yes," he reflected. "They could be called 'Win Words.' "

As the conversation went on, we realized we were having an "Aha!" moment, one of those rare insights into why things happen. We both laughed as I acknowledged that, in fact, I had done the same thing all my life—asked for help.

The truth is, we all ask to get what we want, but some people ask more effectively than others. How about you? Do you ask effectively? Do you have Win Words you apply? Knowing how to ask effectively can make all the difference. Some converted doubters have even commented, "Asking effectively has changed my life! Saved my life!"

The Essentials of Effective Asking

Big R and I were crossing the street on the way to the football game, when we were stopped in the middle of a traffic lane by one of the most ragged, dirty, pitiful-looking panhandlers I have ever encountered. He held out his hand.

"He's begging for money," I blurted impulsively.

"No, I'm not," he growled defensively. Then he shuffled off diagonally across the street, weaving his way through traffic.

"There you have it," my friend said. "The difference between good and bad asking. He was a bad asker, and got nothing. If he had been a good asker, he would not have been defensive. He could have said, 'You look like you're having a good day. I'm having a bad day. Will you help me?' Then he could have ended his pitch with a smile and an open hand. I would have gladly helped him if he had been sincere and honest."

Later, as we drove home after the football game, our discussions continued. We observed that everyone asks for more love, better healthcare, a lower price, a higher salary, fairer treatment, better communication, and ultimately, a heavenly place in eternity. Asking is a way of communicating to achieve a desired goal. Isn't that how we help ourselves and each other daily?

We wondered what the essentials of effective asking actually were. What were the words that create win-win opportunities? On some, we agreed immediately. Others, we debated. And some we discarded. Our final list included five action words that we called Win Words. The word "Win" is used in its broadest sense in this book, meaning simply success by effort. For example: "She has a winning personality," or "The speech won them over," or "We reached a win-win agreement."

Each of these 5 Win Words is identified, explored and graphically illustrated in this Part I. They are the beams of light illuminating the pathway to personal abundance.

To help you better understand and apply the 5 Win Words, each is expanded with observations, short stories, and quotations from many observers. Hopefully, you will be encouraged to expand your thinking and energize what we call your Circle of People and your Circle of Wants. In my 5,000 client experiences, I discovered early that the most memorable impressions flow from experiences requiring thoughtful reflection.

You Don't Have to Reinvent the Wheel

Learn from others' experiences. They offer you the opportunity to find out how to fulfill your wants without enduring the irreversible outcomes of firsthand experience. In other words, you make gains without risking losses. You create win-win opportunities.

Start by comparing and contrasting your own experiences with the observed experiences of others. As these experiences mix and link, as in a chemical reaction, you will find yourself identifying new solutions to old vexing problems.

The New *ASK* Paradigm

A paradigm, in its broadest context, is an explanatory model. The term may be used to describe a set of experiences, beliefs and values that change the way an individual perceives reality and responds to that perception. A paradigm is a pattern that reduces apparent chaos into some form of order.

A simplified analogy for paradigm is a habit of reasoning. It refers to "the box" when we talk about "thinking outside the box"—a phrase that encourages people to engage with a new paradigm. A new paradigm ultimately creates a new box.

The ASK paradigm chart on the following pages illustrates in graphic form how effective people get what they want. It identifies a pattern of thought that reduces an individual's actions and reactions to a form of order. I discovered this pattern by observing 5,000 people seeking to fulfill their needs and desires—their wants.

Each of us tends to think we see things as they are, that we are objective. But this is not the case. We see our world, not as it is, but as we are conditioned to see it by our own experiences. Paradigms are powerful because they become the windows through which we see the world.

Personal paradigms often change as a result of an "Aha!" experience, when someone finally reframes the composite picture in other ways. It's as though a light is suddenly turned on, illuminating a new pathway through a dark forest. The "Aha!" experience with Big R, which inspired this book, changed both our paradigms forever.

Paradigm changes may be instantaneous, or slow and deliberate. Modern medicine is filled with paradigm shifts as new ways of treating cancer, heart disease, flu epidemics, and much more, are put into practice. The concept of marriage for love is a radical departure from the older system of matchmaking by family arrangement. Western democracy is a paradigm away from kings, dictators, and anarchy. The rule of law is vastly different from the old "eye for an eye" system of dispute resolution. Our paradigms, correct or incorrect, are the source of our attitudes and behaviors, and ultimately our relationships with others.

Consider the ASK paradigm as a new box, a set of thought patterns that may be helpful in seeking to achieve your goals. The ASK paradigm is an explanatory model of how to ask effectively.

"Ask" is the foundation, the beginning of the paradigm. The Win Words are the pillars, the supporting connectors that give the model its pattern. "Win" is the capstone, the crowning achievement of the paradigm—getting what you want. In Part I of this book, paradigm illustrations graphically demonstrate the importance of each Win Word to the power of the paradigm.

Computer gurus already have developed "ask" algorithms to identify sets of "ask instructions" that solve technical and mathematical problems. Perhaps cultural algorithms will be developed using the ASK paradigm to help you fulfill your wants.

Persistence is the difference between achievers and everyone else.

PERSISTENCE

Persistence is essential to fulfilling wants. The basis of persistence is the power of determination and will. Willpower transforms desires to reality.

Walter D. Wintle is famous for writing only one piece of literature. Little is known about this late 19th-century man except for the way he inspired future generations with his poem, "The Man Who Thinks He Can."

> If you think you are beaten, you are;
> If you think you dare not, you don't.
> If you'd like to win, but think you can't
> It's almost a cinch you won't.
> If you think you'll lose, you've lost,
> For out in the world we find
> Success being with a fellow's will;
> It's all in the state of mind.
> If you think you're outclassed, you are;
> You've got to think high to rise.

You've got to be sure of yourself before
You can ever win a prize.
Life's battles don't always go
To the stronger or faster man,
But soon or late the man who wins
Is the one who thinks he can.

Steve Jobs' Vision

On June 14, 2005, Steve Jobs, co-founder and CEO of Apple, delivered a very strong speech to the graduating class at Stanford University. The main idea was to show the new graduates how a man of adoptive parents and little money pursued his dreams to become one of the richest men in the world.

"You have to trust that the dots will somehow connect in your future," he observed. "You have to trust in something: your gut, destiny, life, karma, whatever. This approach has never let me down, and it has made all the difference in my life."

Jobs had a defining design philosophy: Simplicity is always the ultimate goal. When planning the Mac computer, iPod, iPhone, and iPad, his engineers said the products could not be simplified. He disagreed—and persisted in encouraging them to design products that were innovative and easy to use. His persistence paid off in new, revolutionary technologies that not only saved Apple from near bankruptcy, but transformed it into the most valuable company in the world.

Steve Jobs was persistent in pursuing what he wanted. He was determined to develop innovative technologies at affordable prices worldwide. His tireless will to win overcame all obstacles. And while his story is now legendary, other examples of persistence prove life-changing every day.

Leah Gets the Part

"Tell me a teenage story about persistence," I invited during a conversation with 16-year-old Martha.

She replied, "Do you know the story of Anne Frank?"

"Yes," I replied, confident that I knew where Martha was headed. Certainly, Anne Frank's The Diary of a Young Girl told an unforgettable World War II-era story of persistence.

"Her book was required reading in my literature class. We discussed it a lot. I'll never forget her story. Without knowing if she was going to live or die, she kept writing. She never gave up. She was persistent.

"But," Martha said to my surprise, "that's not the persistence I'm thinking about." She continued:

> Anne Frank's diary has been made into a play, which was presented at our Christian School. Anne was Jewish. Leah, a girl in the class who had never acted before, was determined to play the part of Anne Frank. She asked the teacher who was directing the production if she could have the role, but the teacher wasn't encouraging. There were several more experienced students who also wanted the part.
> Leah got really emotional about it. She kept talking about human rights and religious rights. She memorized the entire script for the tryout. She studied how Anne looked, how her family lived in hidden rooms of her father's office building for over two years. Finally, the teacher relented and selected Leah for the role. She was great in the play and got a standing ovation. She lived the part. She is now giving talks to classes in other schools about Anne Frank and even dresses up like her for the talks. I'd call Leah persistent.

I agree. Leah prepared herself. When the right time came, she asked earnestly for the part of Anne Frank. After being selected, she became determined to make her performance memorable. And she succeeded.

A New Family Partnership

Persistence takes many forms. It plays a vital part in the give-and-take of daily affairs. Big R again comes to mind. As a real estate salesman earning commissions, he was resolute in his work. If he could fairly match a customer's wants to a particular property, he would work days, nights, and weekends until the seller, buyer, and lender signed the closing papers. Good salespeople are a little bit like movie stars: Once talent meets opportunity, the money flows.

I watched as Big R began to invest in real estate himself and accumulated capital. I thought to myself, "I can do that, too—make my living during the week practicing law and work nights and weekends on my own small investments. All I need is determination."

I put a small classified ad in the newspaper: "Investor looking for real estate opportunity," with a post office box. I received mostly form letter responses—all except one. A handwritten note on lined paper said, "My brother knows a widowed woman who lives by herself in a mobile home on one hundred acres of land. She wants to sell and move to Phoenix."

I called and then met the young man who wrote the note, then his brother, and finally the widow. I listened to her story, and I was honest. "I have very little money," I explained to her. At first, that seemed to end the conversation, but I believed we could make a win-win deal satisfying her needs and goals.

If she would finance the sale, I suggested, we could work together. She could move to Phoenix immediately and return to her mobile home in Black Forest, north of Colorado Springs, to enjoy the beautiful summers. Eventually, we agreed to a win-win deal. For five years we worked together as I subdivided the land into 19 appealing five-acre properties with a country road curving through the middle of the tract.

Slowly, the lots sold. I paid the kind widow the remaining money I owed her, plus interest, and kept the lot with her mobile home maintained for her, all expenses paid, until she decided not to return.

The development was called New Discovery. I created a family partnership with the same name. My wife and three children were—and still are—the partners. Over the years, the partnership has bought and sold other real estate properties, and the assets have grown. The profits have helped send our three children through college, graduate schools, and professional schools. New Discovery now owns a historic ranch where our grandchildren learn about nature, work fixing fences, fish, hunt and enjoy exploring the forests, pasture, hayfields, lakes and streams. I've told them the story of New Discovery. Maybe they will learn the value of persistence from that story.

Powerful Observations about Persistence:

"Suppose one of you shall have a friend and shall go to him at midnight and say to him, 'Friend, lend me three loaves; for a friend of mine has come to me from a journey, and I have nothing to set before him;' and from inside he shall answer and say, 'Do not bother me; the door has already been shut, and my children and I are in bed; I cannot get up and give you anything.' I tell you, even though he will not get up and give him anything because he is his friend, yet because of his persistence he will get up and give him as much as he needs. And I say to you, ask, and it shall be given to

you; seek, and you shall find; knock, and it shall be opened to you. For everyone o asks, receives; and he who seeks, finds; and to him who knocks, it shall be opened."
—Bible, Luke 11:5-10

"Never confuse a single defeat with a final defeat."
—F. Scott Fitzgerald, author

"Champions aren't made in gyms. Champions are made from something they have deep inside them—a desire, a dream, a vision. They have to have last-minute stamina, they have to be a little faster, they have to have the skill and the will. But the will must be stronger than the skill."
—Muhammad Ali, world heavyweight champion boxer

"When things go wrong, don't go with them."
—Elvis Presley, singer

It even helps stupid people to try hard."
—Lucius Annaeus Seneca, philosopher

"Life's a bitch. You've got to go out and kick ass."
—Maya Angelou, author

"Nothing in this world can take the place of persistence. Talent will not; nothing is more common than unsuccessful people with talent."
—Calvin Coolidge, U.S. president

"Do not be too timid and squeamish about your actions. All life is an experiment. The more experiments you make the better. What if they are a little coarse and you may get your coat soiled or torn? What if you do fail and get fairly rolled in the dirt once or twice?

Up again, you shall never be so afraid of a tumble."
—Ralph Waldo Emerson, essayist and philosopher

"Do you not know that in a race all the runners run, but only one receives the prize. So run that you may obtain it."
—Bible, I Corinthians 9:24

"My motto was always to keep swinging. Whether I was in a slump or feeling badly or having trouble off the field, the only thing to do was keep swinging."
—Hank Aaron, Hall of Fame baseball player

"Leaders aren't born, they are made. And they are made just like anything else, through hard work. And that's the price we'll have to pay to achieve that goal, or any goal."
—Vince Lombardi, Hall of Fame football coach

"It's easy to make a buck. It's a lot tougher to make a difference."
—Tom Brokaw, news broadcaster

"An invincible determination can accomplish almost anything, and in this lies the great distinction between great men and little men."
—Thomas Fuller, English churchman and historian

"A winner is someone who recognizes his God-given talents, works his tail off to develop them into skills, and uses these skills to accomplish his goals."
—Larry Bird, Hall of Fame basketball player

"To finish first, you must first finish."
—Rick Mears, race car driver

"Paralyze resistance with persistence."
—Woody Hayes, Hall of Fame college football coach

Appreciative words and gestures of commitment are expressions of sincerity.

SINCERITY

Sincerity is another way of saying that you mean what you say and act accordingly. If you mean what you say, you're sincere. If you don't, you're not. Sincerity is a characteristic we value. We love to find it in other people, and we love it when other people find it in us.

Sincerity may be the most controversial of the Win Words because it's so open to interpretation. If someone acts according to the dictates of his conscience, we recognize his sincerity—he's being true to himself. But this understanding has weaknesses. One can sincerely believe in a false idea, and this belief may stand in the way of progress. For example, someone might say, "My country's culture is the best in the world." Many wars have been fought, and millions have died, as people worked from this "sincere" premise.

In my law practice, I've seen that people sometimes believe, in all sincerity, that their spouse is the cause of all their problems. But the problems they encounter in life, the blocks to their success, are really centered in themselves. People can even be sincerely foolish. Sincerely wrong.

Sincerity, as a Win Word, may have its ambiguities. However,

Big R believes this word best expresses the importance of positive communication. To be liked or loved, we must be sincere.

Dr. Milt's Personal Side

Here are two stories that Dr. Milt, a client, friend and orthopedic surgeon, told me that illustrate the real value of sincerity.

> I was filling my gas tank at a local convenience store when a middle-aged man hesitantly approached me, holding a one-gallon orange plastic gasoline container. "Excuse me," he said. "We've run out of gas. We had to push the car to the curb, and we don't have any money. Times have been kind of tough lately. Could you help us by filling this container?"
>
> At a glance, he seemed clean, calm, and nonthreatening. I could see a woman sitting in his 1980s faded-blue van, which was parked at an angle against the curb. Without hesitation, I put the hose nozzle into his open can and filled it up. As he shuffled back to his car, he said unexpectedly, "Thank you, and God bless."
>
> "Come back, and I'll fill it up again," I replied. He returned for five more gallons.
>
> Why did I help this stranger? Because he was sincere. His appreciation reaffirmed his sincerity. I really couldn't say no. And frankly, helping him made me feel good all day.
>
> I remember another occasion, when I was buying a used car. I was feeling a little tense going into the dealership, expecting some pushy salesperson to pounce. But that didn't happen. Instead, the salesman who introduced himself was very low-key. He greeted me with a friendly handshake and direct eye contact. He asked how he could be of help. I told him I was

looking to replace a car for my wife. He asked me about her and the rest of my family, explaining that it would help him understand what kind of vehicle I might be looking for. He didn't try to rush things. He took time to answer all my questions. I felt he had a sincere desire to learn what it was that I wanted and needed. He didn't seem to be selling me a car. He was allowing me to buy.

As our conversation went on, I learned more about him. I still remember his name: Chuck Zimmer. Chuck had been selling cars and trucks for 23 years, 10 years at that dealership. It had paid for his kids' college education. Last year, he had stepped down from a sales manager's position so he could spend more time on the lot dealing directly with customers. He loved his work.

A week later, after visiting several other used car lots, my wife and I returned and purchased a vehicle from Chuck. How could we not? His sincerity had sold us. Even when he had asked directly for something from us, it was for information that would ultimately make our buying experience more satisfying. That's effective asking at its very best.

Coach Calhoun's Commitment

Troy Calhoun is the coach of the Falcons, the Air Force Academy football team. He is an Air Force Academy graduate himself. Since he returned to the Academy in 2007, the Falcons have enjoyed a sustained run of success.

One season early in his tenure, Air Force beat both Navy and Army, winning the Commander-in-Chief's Trophy. They closed out the season by beating Georgia Tech in the Independence Bowl. Afterward, Calhoun said in an interview:

I ask my players for complete commitment on the field and in the classroom. Our team is like a family. There's an unbreakable bond between teammates and coaches. We are responsible to ourselves and to each other. It's a duty of excellence.

My father, like any good father, taught me words carry weight only when transported into reality by action. Dad didn't talk much. Didn't have time to talk much. He was busy backing up his words.

When Calhoun came to coach the Falcons, his résumé included work as an assistant coach in the National Football League, with the Denver Broncos and the Houston Texans. Along the way, he decided to pass on at least one NFL head-coaching offer, as well as offers from higher-paying college programs. Those decisions cost him several million dollars, but as one of his former players has observed, "It's not about the money to him. It's about quality of life. He gets to spend more time with family here than he ever would in the NFL. He gets to work with quality guys like us from the Academy. We realize how much he cares about us. If he was willing to turn down that much money to stay here, to coach this specific group of guys, he is going to inspire us."

Calhoun is asking for top performance from his players. He can do that effectively because they have seen what he is willing to sacrifice to remain true to himself. They have faith in his integrity—another word for sincerity.

Powerful Observations about Sincerity:

"A friend is a person with whom I may be sincere. Before him, I may think aloud."
—Ralph Waldo Emerson, American lecturer, essayist, and poet

"But the goal of our instruction is love from a pure heart and a good conscience and a sincere faith."
—Bible, I Timothy 1:15

"Sincerity and truth are the basis of every virtue."
—Confucius, Chinese philosopher

"You desire and do not have; so you kill. And you covet and cannot obtain; so you fight and wage war. You do not have, because you do not ask. You ask and do not receive, because you ask wrongly, to spend it on your passions."
—Bible, James 4:2-3

"A man who views the world the same at fifty as he did at twenty has wasted thirty years of his life."
—Muhammad Ali, world heavyweight champion boxer

"It takes a lot of courage to show your dreams to someone else."
—Erma Bombeck, syndicated columnist

"You know I say just what I think, and nothing more nor less—I cannot say one thing and mean another."
—Henry Wadsworth Longfellow, American poet and educator

"Sincerity is to speak as we think, to do as we pretend and profess, to perform what we promise, and really to be what we would seem and appear to be."
—John Tillotson, Archbishop of Canterbury

"The man with a message is a whole lot harder to listen to."
—Will Rogers, author and cowboy humorist

"When the heart is right, the mind and the body will follow."
—Coretta Scott King, civil rights activist

"I have never considered a difference of opinion in politics, in religion, in philosophy, as a cause for withdrawing from a friendship."
—Thomas Jefferson, U.S. president

"You will, undoubtedly, meet people who will try to shut you up or entice you to compromise your principles in any number of ways. They'll try to seduce you and distract you with money, power, security and perhaps, most dangerously, a sense of belonging. Don't let them; it's just not worth it."
—Samuel L. Jackson, actor

"A good heart is better than all the heads in the world."
—Edward Bulwer-Lytton, English politician, poet, playwright

"You make a living by what you get; you make a life by what you give."
—Winston Churchill, British prime minister

"Sincerity is always subject to proof."
—John F. Kennedy, U.S. president

"Begin somewhere. You cannot build a reputation on what you intend to do."
—Liz Smith, columnist

"Every day is a gift—even if it sucks."
—Sherry Hochman, author

"Be sincere, be brief, be seated."
—Franklin D. Roosevelt, U.S. president

"Sincerity is the biggest part of selling anything—including the Christian plan of salvation."
—Billy Graham, evangelist

Humility changes rivals into supporters and friends.

HUMILITY

In an effort to express the meaning of humility—our next Win Word—in very simple terms, I wrote the following whimsical poem when my children were small. To my surprise, each of them memorized it and used it in school. Other people started requesting copies. It has been published on wallet cards and bookmarks in libraries.

Rubber Bands

Answers to the World's demand,
May be found in rubber bands.

Shot thru the air, kicked on the ground,
They give and take without a sound.

They lie and hang around the room,
Hoping to be useful soon.

Throughout the day they stretch and bend,
With full response that has no end.

> Their life is insecure and tense,
> All work is without recompense.
>
> They go the limit—never stop,
> They strain until they win—or pop.

Too much ego exaggerates our own importance in the world and can make us intolerant, dismissive, or disrespectful toward others. Its opposite, humility, makes us nimble and adaptable, opens our hearts, and prepares us for the road ahead, no matter how tough it may be. Here are some stories that illustrate what I mean.

Jessica Leads by Example

Elizabeth, a 16-year-old high school sophomore, once told me a story about humility that I've never forgotten.

> Jessica is two years ahead of me in school. We have become friends playing on the same club soccer team. Our moms carpool to practice and games. We talk a lot in the back seat while we're traveling.
> She was selected to play on the travel team and misses classes when she plays in out-of-state tournaments, but she has a super high grade point average. When I ask, she gives me advice on the field and helps me become a better soccer player. She also helps me with my algebra when we're riding home in the van after practice. She never expects anything in return.
> We are in the same chemistry class. One session, we took a hard mid-term exam. The next day, we received

back our graded tests. I was penalized three points for a wrong answer. I read the question again. My answer still seemed right. Jessica and I compared answers. She had lost three points for giving the same answer.

Jessica observed that the question was ambiguous, allowing for two correct answers, including ours. She immediately went into action, personally asking the teacher to reconsider making both answers correct. After re-reading the question several times, and listening to Jessica's explanation, the teacher agreed. Most of the class got three more points on the test. It raised my score from a B to an A. No one ever knew Jessica's initiative made the difference.

She's probably the most popular girl in school—mostly because she's so humble. She never brags. She's never in your face. I want to be like Jessica. This summer, we're planning to run a 5K race together to help raise money for diabetes research. I hope we can still continue our friendship after she goes away to college.

One of the most important questions you can ever ask yourself is, "Do I want to brag, or do I want to be humble?" Often, the two choices produce opposite results. Being aggressive, arrogant, impetuous—all branches of the same in-your-face tree—takes an enormous amount of mental energy and often alienates us from loved ones, friends, and co-workers.

Do you know an "I'm always right" assertive person? In the midst of a disagreement, consider saying, "You are right. Thank you for correcting me." Who's right or wrong probably won't make a difference in anyone's life. Most disputes are opinion-driven. So why not try another strategy? In the spirit of humility, take the path less traveled.

Problems Include Opportunities

After the birth of our first child, when our growing family needed more room both under our roof and outside, my wife noticed a classified ad in the local newspaper. The headline read: "For those who want an estate and can't afford one." That was us.

We responded to the ad and looked at the property. It was definitely a fixer-upper. The only positives we both agreed on were the family-perfect location and the large lot. While I saw only problems, my wife declared it an opportunity. I resisted taking an "I'm right, you're wrong" attitude and agreed to negotiate with the seller.

Reluctantly, I made a ridiculously low offer—which the seller immediately accepted. What I did not know at the time was that the seller was in ugly disputes with two adjacent neighbors. One claimed the seller had built a fence three feet into the neighbor's yard. They were fighting it out in court. The other claimed the driveway crossed his property; he had a stack of cinder blocks and was threatening to build a wall across the driveway.

The seller said he was right and the neighbors were wrong. He was sick of fighting them and wanted to move. Later, I learned that his wife also felt sick of his "I'm right, you're wrong" attitude. She had filed for divorce.

Before closing on the purchase, I reviewed the boundary surveys and concluded that both neighbors were more right than wrong. I knocked on the door of the first neighbor, ate humble pie, suggested he was right, and offered to move the fence. He smiled, we shook hands, and he agreed to help with the work. We became fast friends.

I visited the second neighbor and acknowledged the driveway did cross his property. He admitted it had been there as long as he owned the property and was probably a legal right-of-way. He referred to the seller as that "crazy bird on the hill," a guy who left trash on the driveway. I offered to clean up the trash and create an easement to define everyone's rights. We shook hands and have never had a cross word, then or since.

We bought the house at a very low cost by refusing to indulge in the "I'm right, you're wrong" neighborhood game. My wife was right: A hidden opportunity had lurked within what had seemed a mountain of troubles. Buying a home that was in such poor condition required humility, but in return, we got the place at a great price. Being humble and effectively asking for a new start with the neighbors had also cleared the way for valuable new relationships.

The challenge is to allow others the joy of being right—without being run over. In my law practice, I try to achieve my clients' goals with the least amount of confrontation. It's not always easy. If everyone were humble, we would not need lawyers. And, of course, sometimes there really is a clear right and a clear wrong. When there are indisputable facts or philosophical positions that require firm positions, explain them to anyone who will listen.

But most times, right-versus-wrong arguments are about opinions, not facts. If someone says something you disagree with, instead of arguing, just let it go. You will give someone else validation, which in turn, will make you feel good. You don't have to sacrifice your own principles in the process. You're not giving up your values. You're just allowing someone else to have their moment. With humility, you will be surprised how quickly potential adversaries become friends and supporters.

Powerful Observations about Humility:

"I've missed more than 9,000 shots in my career. I've lost almost 300 games; 26 times, I've been trusted to take the game winning shot and missed. I've failed over and over and over again in my life. And that is why I succeed."

—Michael Jordan, Hall of Fame basketball player

"If you hear that someone is speaking ill of you, instead of trying to defend yourself, you should say, 'He obviously does not know me very well, since there are so many other faults he could have mentioned.'"
—Epictetus, philosopher

"You don't have to be a 'person of influence' to be influential. In fact, the most influential people in my life are probably not even aware of the things they've taught me."
—Scott Adams, cartoonist and creator of "Dilbert" comic strip

"When pride comes, then comes disgrace, but with the humble is wisdom."
—Bible, Proverbs 11:2

"Real integrity is doing the right thing, knowing that nobody is going to know whether you did it or not."
—Oprah Winfrey, media magnate

"I think you should take your job seriously, but not yourself—that is the best combination."
—Judi Dench, actress

"The best way to destroy an enemy is to make him your friend."
—Abraham Lincoln, U.S. President

"The greatest weakness of all weaknesses is to fear too much to appear weak."
—Jacques Bénigne Bossuet, bishop and theologian

"Success is going from failure to failure without a loss of enthusiasm."
—Winston Churchill, British prime minister

"I am a little deaf, a little blind, a little impotent, and on top of this are two or three abominable infirmities, but nothing destroys my hope."
—Francois Marie Arouet Voltaire, philosopher and writer

"Keep your eyes open and your mouth shut."
—John Steinbeck, author

"Flops are part of life's menu."
—Rosalind Russell, actress

"Life's most urgent question is: What are you doing for others?"
—Martin Luther King, Jr., civil rights leader

"Contrary to the cliché, genuinely nice guys most often finish first or very near it."
—Malcolm Forbes, publisher

"I cannot think that we are useless, or God would not have created us."
—Geronimo, Apache leader

"Use power to help people. For we are given power not to advance our own purposes, nor to make a great show in the world, nor a name. There is but one just use of power and it is to serve people."
—George H.W. Bush, U.S. president

"It is amazing what you can accomplish if you do not care who gets the credit."
—Harry S. Truman, U.S. president

When you are honest with yourself and others you will be respected.

HONESTY

Billy Joel was the first U.S. pop star to bring a full stage production to Moscow. Among other accomplishments, he has received Grammy Awards for Record of the Year, Song of the Year, Album of the Year, and Male Pop Vocal Performance, and has received the Grammys' Legend Award. He has performed at two Super Bowls. He has sold more than 150 million albums.

Billy Joel's "Honesty" lyrics are perhaps his most memorable, as evidenced by the sheer number of people who have downloaded the lyrics onto their cell phones and computers. His lyrics begin:

> If you search for tenderness
> It isn't hard to find.
> You can have the love you need to live.
> But if you look for truthfulness
> You might just as well be blind.
> It always seems to be so hard to give.
> Honesty is such a lonely word.
> Everyone is so untrue.
> Honesty is hardly ever heard.
> And mostly what I need from you.

Honesty is a part of everything we say and do. We are judged hourly by our credibility at home, in the workplace, and socially.

Only when we are honest with ourselves can we be honest with others. We are all both leaders and followers. If we lead with half-truths and exaggerations, others will follow. If we follow others who misrepresent facts, we will do the same. In court, witnesses are required to swear under oath to "tell the truth, the whole truth, and nothing but the truth." The oath repeats the word "truth" three times. No option is available for half-truths or exaggerations. On the witness stand, life-changing decisions depend upon the truth.

A Soldier Wins in Court

In my early career as a counselor-at-law, I often represented indigent defendants charged with serious crimes. My job was to plead my client's case before a judge or jury, to present the evidence most favorable to proving my client's innocence. The district attorney's duty was to prosecute, to present evidence showing my client was guilty as charged.

In one unpredictable case, I was appointed by the court to represent a Mr. Stewart. He was an enlisted soldier from Fort Carson in Colorado who could not afford to hire and pay an attorney. A public defender attorney was not available. Mr. Stewart was charged with theft and forgery, each felony punishable by five years in the state penitentiary. He allegedly stole, and signed someone else's name on, a personal check. He claimed innocence.

The district attorney presented the state's evidence, including a handwriting expert, to testify that the signature on the check was my client's handwriting, and a blurred photo of a man wearing sunglasses and a baseball cap passing a Burger King payroll check at a supermarket to purchase groceries. The supermarket clerk testified he believed the person in the blurred photo was my client. However, he was not 100 percent sure. My own handwriting expert refuted the prosecution's expert.

As we left the courtroom after the second day of trial, my client and I were both discouraged. He was out of jail on bond.

As we waited for the elevator, a courthouse employee asked if he could talk to me. He seemed nervous, hesitant. His voice barely rose above a mumble. "I don't want to bring any trouble on myself," he said. "I don't like to get involved in these things. But I have to be honest. It's the only way I can stay right with myself and right with the Lord."

"It's okay," I reassured him. "You're not going to get into any trouble for being honest. But this man standing next to me is looking at many years in prison, and if you can in any way help him, I would ask that you do that."

"Well," he said, "During a recess of the trial, I went into the courtroom and looked at the photo on the evidence table. I know who that is!" he blurted.

"Who?" I stammered.

"He used to be a janitor in the county office administration building across the street. He stole some checks from Burger King. He mentioned it one evening after a few beers."

"Are you sure?" I queried.

"Very sure."

The next day, I called the courthouse employee as our final witness. He took the stand and took an oath to tell the truth.

I handed him the photo and asked if he could identify the person.

He gave the man's name without hesitation. "Leroy Polk," he said.

"How do you know this man?" I asked him.

"He's a former employee at the county office building across the street. I knew him for a couple of years."

"Where is this man now?"

"Shot and killed in a bar in Wichita Falls, Texas, last year," he said with a sigh.

"No further questions," I concluded.

The jury deliberated less than two hours before finding my client not guilty. He had asked for justice. And another man had given it to him through his honesty.

In my professional practice, I have found honesty in personal relationships to be an extraordinary challenge. Confronting change, making decisions by action or default, and honestly communicating about these experiences all redirect lives every day.

The following family story illustrates challenges in honestly responding when someone asks for help.

Molly Sobbed

Molly opened the envelope and pulled out a single sheet of paper.

> Dear Mrs. Hemming:
>
> I am a court appointed intermediary, acting on behalf of Ethan Best. According to court records, Mr. Best is the child you gave up for adoption in 1975. Mr. Best is now requesting to talk to you if you wish. Barring that, he would appreciate family medical information.
> If you would like to speak with Mr. Best I will be happy to arrange a meeting. If you do not wish to do so, that is your choice.
> Please let me know.
>
> Sincerely,
> Denise Stroud

Molly collapsed heavily into a chair, tears streaming down her face. "Oh, not now," she sobbed. "I can't do this now." Tucking the letter in her purse, she began cooking supper. The kitchen door banged as her husband, Gary, stormed in.

"What a day. If those idiots don't get the contracts finished soon, I'm going to fire them all. What's for supper? Spaghetti again? Can't you cook anything else?" He extracted a beer from the refrigerator.

Did you call my sister?"

"N-n-no, was I supposed to?"

"I told you, they want us to come over for dinner tomorrow night and talk about Ma."

Molly placed a huge plate of spaghetti in front of her husband.

I'm sorry. I'll do it tomorrow."

"Do it now," Gary roared.

Later, Molly sat in the dark, remembering the night Ethan was born. Ethan, that was a nice name. She had named him after her dad, knowing it would be changed. The baby's father was in the U.S. Army. She was barely out of high school and her father said he was not raising another child. Molly sadly left the baby with a children's home for adoption.

Now she had the chance to see him, to get to know him. Did he favor her dad's dark eyes and curly hair, or his own father's blond hair and blue eyes? He had never been out of her thoughts, but Gary had never wanted children and she knew he would not accept her son into their family. Nor, she knew, would his family.

The next day, Molly called Denise. Barely containing her tears, she told the intermediary that she could not talk to Mr. Best at this time, but she would furnish family medical information. "Please tell him," she said, "that I had no choice but to give him up, and I have no choice now."

"Would it be alright if he sent you a letter?" Denise asked.

"Yes, but please send it care of my sister, Janet Woodridge, at 1000 Sands Road."

"I'll do that, Mrs. Hemming."

Three weeks later, Janet called. "Molly, you have a letter from a Mason Best. Shall I bring it over?"

"No, I'll be right there."

Molly hurried to her sister's and snatched the letter from her. "Molly, what's all the mystery?" Janet asked.

"This is from my son."

"Your son? Oh my. Sweetie, are you okay?"

"Yes, but you know I can't tell anyone else."

"Read the letter, Molly."

The letter Mason had written to his birth mother emphasized that he understood her reluctance to meet with him, and said he had received the family health information she had provided through Denise Stroud.

"I just want you to know that I have a good life," he said. "I am married and you have three grandchildren. The reason I am contacting you now is that my oldest daughter, who is only 17, is pregnant and is considering adoption. We are willing to support her decision, whatever it might be. I am certain you gave me up for adoption because it was either your only option or the best you could give me. I want Lela to have more choices.

"Thank you for giving me life and if you ever want to get in touch with me in the future, I would like to get to know you."

Janet read the letter as Molly sobbed, then hugged her sister tightly.

"Janet, I can't help him. I just hope Lela makes the right decision, one she can live with the rest of her life."

"Tell her that, Molly. Write to her and tell her in your own honest, heartfelt way that you've been in her shoes and tell her that you would have liked to keep your baby. Tell her honestly how you felt when you gave your son up for adoption, and how you feel now."

As soon as Gary left for work the next day, Molly sat down to write. "My dearest Lela ..."

Powerful Observations about Honesty:

"The truth always turns out to be simpler than you thought."
—Richard Feynman, American physicist

"If your success is not on your own terms, if it looks good to the world but does not feel good in your heart, it is not success at all."
—Anna Quindlen, Pulitzer Prize-winning journalist

"Honesty is the first chapter in the book of wisdom."
—Thomas Jefferson, U.S. president

"Nobody is always a winner, and anybody who says he is, is either a liar or doesn't play poker."
—George Orwell, author

"Confidence ... thrives on honesty, on honor, on the sacredness of obligations, on faithful protection and on unselfish performance. Without them it cannot live."
—Franklin D. Roosevelt, U.S. president

"Little children, let us not love with word or with tongue, but in deed and truth."
—Bible, I John 3:18

"A man's reputation is the opinion people have of him; his character is what he really is."
—Jack Miner, Canadian conservationist

"I have found no greater satisfaction than achieving success through honest dealing and strict adherence to the view that, for you to gain, those you deal with should gain as well."
—Alan Greenspan, American economist and former chairman of the Federal Reserve

"I think we all have a little voice inside us that will guide us. It may be God, I don't know. But I think that if we shut out all the noise and clutter from our lives and listen to that voice, it will tell us the right thing to do."
—Christopher Reeve, actor

"I am very little inclined on any occasion to say anything unless I hope to produce some good by it."
—Abraham Lincoln, U.S. president

"If you don't have enemies, you don't have character."
—Paul Newman, actor

"The future turns out to be something that you make instead of find. It isn't waiting for your arrival, either with an arrest warrant or a band, nor is it any farther away than the next sentence, the next best guess, the next sketch for the painting of a life portrait that might become a masterpiece. The future is an empty canvas or a blank sheet of paper, and if you have the courage of your own thought and your own observation, you can make of it what you will."
—Lewis Lapham, American writer and editor

"I submit to you that if a man hasn't discovered something that he will die for, he isn't fit to live."
—Martin Luther King Jr., civil rights activist

"And you will know the truth, and the truth shall set you free."
—Bible, I John 8:32

"Your time is limited, so don't waste it living someone else's life. Don't be trapped by dogma—which is living with the results of other people's thinking. Don't let the noise of others' opinions drown out your own inner voice. And most important, have the courage to follow your heart and intuition. They somehow already know what you truly want to become. Everything else is secondary."
—Steve Jobs, co-founder and CEO of Apple

"I've come to believe that each of us has a personal calling that's as unique as a fingerprint and that the best way to succeed is to discover what you love and then find a way to offer it to others in the form of service, working hard, and also allowing the energy of the universe to lead you."
—Oprah Winfrey, media magnate

"Honesty and integrity are absolutely essential in life—all areas of life. The really good news is that anyone can develop both honesty and integrity."
—Zig Ziglar, motivational speaker

"I believe fundamental honesty is the keystone of business."
—Harvey S. Firestone, businessman

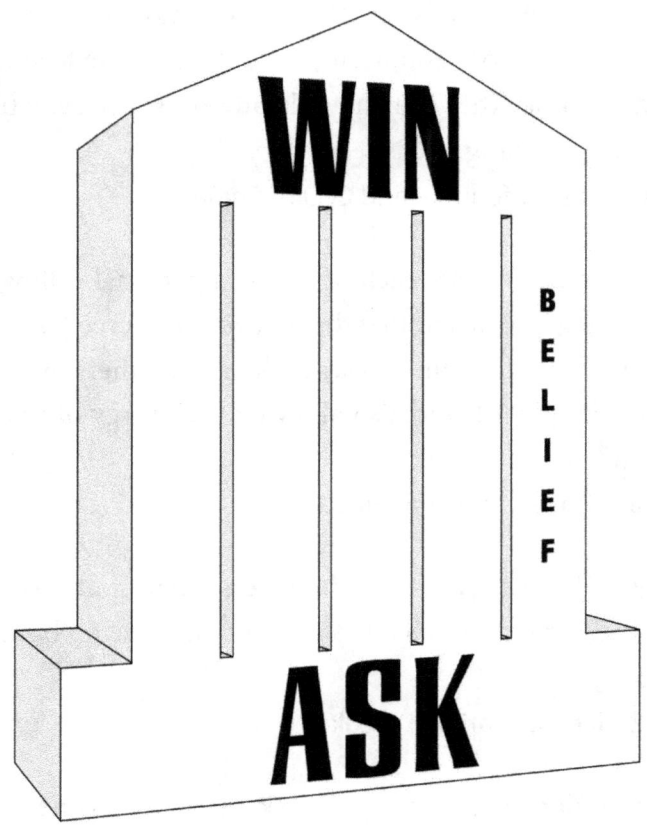

Belief teaches anything is possible.

BELIEF

John Stewart Mill, a philosopher and political economist, observed, "One person with a belief is equal to a force of 99 who have only interests." That is exactly why beliefs fling open the door to becoming super-effective. Beliefs can be the most powerful forces for fulfilling wants. Conversely, beliefs that limit your actions and thoughts can be devastating.

Religious and scientific beliefs have both empowered and divided millions of people throughout history. Today's headlines are often driven by life-and-death decisions based on religious and scientific beliefs. The people who have changed history—Christ, Mohammad, Copernicus, Luther, Einstein—have been the people who have changed our beliefs.

You can consciously model your beliefs by reading and viewing biographies of great leaders. Abraham Lincoln is a favorite. He suffered many setbacks: His mother died when he was 9 years old, only one of his four children lived into adulthood, he was defeated in political elections, and suffered bouts of depression. Yet he became the most effective president in United States history, winning the Civil War, freeing the slaves, creating a national banking system, and institutionalizing homesteading in the West. Lincoln justified the horrific loss of life in the Civil War with his belief of the sanctity of personal liberty and equality. He expressed this in the beginning of his famous Gettysburg Address:

> Four score and seven years ago, our Fathers brought forth on this Continent, a new nation, conceived in liberty, and dedicated to the proposition that all men are created equal.

On a personal level, we are all aware of the placebo effect. Drug companies often experiment with new drugs by giving one group of people the new drug, and another an identical-looking pill with no active properties. One remarkable placebo study concerned a group of patients with acid reflux and heartburn. The first group was given a pill and advised it was a new drug that would absolutely produce relief. The second group was given a pill and told it was an experimental drug but very little was known of its effects. In fact, in both cases, the patients received a pill with no medicinal properties.

Seventy percent of the first group experienced significant relief from their conditions. Only 25 percent of the second group experienced relief. There are hundreds of studies using placebo pills with similar outcomes. Studies show that the reactions to drugs correspond closely to expectations.

A thought, when nurtured to a belief, is like an apple seed. Planted in fertile soil and nurtured, it can germinate and grow to become a lush object of value and beauty. The original seed of an idea may be planted in the mind through repetitious thought. That is why you are encouraged to write down your wants, commit them to memory, and repeat them by writing them day after day, until you believe you will fulfill them.

Somewhere in your mind lie the dormant seeds needed to fulfill your wants. If nourished with belief, these seeds will bear fruit in your life more bountiful than you may ever have believed possible. How? Belief removes limitations, whether it's belief in yourself or belief in the infinite. Belief is the starting point of asking effectively. Belief gives ideas their life and power and turns them into actions. Making repeated affirmations to your subconscious mind will develop the power of belief.

If you believe you will be effective, you will be empowered to achieve. If you believe that you will fail, you will tend to experience failure. You can choose beliefs that limit you, or you can choose beliefs that support you. The challenge is to choose the beliefs that are conducive to effectiveness and the results you want, while discarding the beliefs that hold you back. Belief gives us confidence to move forward even though we don't always know what we'll encounter beyond the next bend.

Who Am I?

Always ask yourself the fundamental question, "Who am I?" You must decide and live life accordingly. Inner strengths that we need to be effective, flow from our answers to this question. We become who we believe we are. Know who you are, and who you want to be. If these images are one and the same, hold fast; if these images vary, consider change.

For many years, Allan Asher and I practiced law together as partners. He was Jewish. I am a committed Christian. We remained fast friends after his retirement. When he, and later his wife, passed on, I was asked to be the attorney in both estates. It was a compliment I treasure.

One of my favorite stories, told to me by a client, best illustrates the basic belief question, "Who am I?"

I was 55 when I learned I was Jewish. Born in San Francisco and raised by my physician parents as a Catholic with private-school background, I was stunned when my brother, Michael, told me, after our mother's funeral, that our parents were Jewish.

Michael explained, "During World War II in Austria, in order to protect themselves from the Nazis, they changed their names, became Catholic, and eliminated all traces of their Jewish background. After the war, they moved to San Francisco, had two children, and began a new life. They never told you or me they were Jewish. Just before our mother's death, she told me the truth, and made me promise not to tell you while she was alive."

I reacted with disbelief and anger. How could it be that I had been lied to all of my life? I was not who I thought I was. How could my parents have done such a thing to their children? For what possible reason?

I became obsessed with finding answers. Michael and I sifted through our mother's belongings looking for anything that might provide information. In a small, locked trunk, we found letters from an unknown uncle and two cousins, and a small address book.

I wondered what I would tell my husband, and our children. One evening, without preamble, I simply announced, "By the way, I just found out I'm Jewish." Everyone laughed. How funny. Stunned silence followed.

I explained what little I knew, and after a slew of questions from the family, my husband suggested I research my genealogy and contact the uncle who still lived in Vienna. With my family's blessing and support, I embarked on a mission of discovery to Austria.

I spent four weeks traveling the country, following a trail of relatives totally unknown to me. I stayed in their homes, asked endless questions, and learned that they all knew of my parents' deceptive identity and had kept their secret. These people who once might have been family were friendly and kind, but no familial warmth was shown to me. I tried hard to connect with them and understand their dynamics, but I couldn't. I was an outcast. I didn't belong.

"Who am I?" I asked my uncle.

"You are the sum of all the things you have lived and experienced. Finding out that your parents were Jewish won't change that. It will only add another dimension. You can't reinvent yourself into being Jewish. Consider that your life has been enriched by this detour in the road." He looked at me kindly. "Our blood may run in your veins, Alicia, but it won't change who you are."

Back home, I was in emotional disarray as my family listened attentively and tried to be sympathetic. But this wasn't about them, so they couldn't possibly understand. Wrong.

"This means we're Jewish, too, right?" my daughter asked with overtones of shock. "Does that mean we're not Catholic anymore?"

"Do we now go to Temple? Celebrate Hanukkah? Have you thought about any of this?" my son wanted to know.

I was stunned by their response. They were worried about religious belief, not race, or culture, or family ties. "Yes, you're part Jewish, too, just as you are a fine stew of

Irish and Italian.

"And of course we're not going to Temple. Why would you think that? I am who I am, and you are still who you are. And we're all Catholic. Subject closed."

Everyone relaxed. Tension melted. Soon they were able to talk about the new branch on the family tree as an amazing serendipity. And during the holidays, a small, symbolic menorah brightens a corner of the room not far from the Nativity. It seems fitting.

We are all born into differing beliefs, races, and cultures. To be an effective asker, we must understand our own birth conditions and the birth conditions of others.

This can best be done by reaching out. Be a good listener. Take into consideration others' beliefs as you develop your own. Manage the beliefs you cannot change.

Louie's Flashback

Laura Hillenbrand's 2010 bestseller, Unbroken, compellingly tells the story of Louis "Louie" Zamperini. In the spring of 1943, Louie's Army Air Force bomber crashed into the Pacific Ocean and disappeared. Along with two other airmen, he survived, struggled to a life raft, and pulled himself aboard — thus beginning a 2½-year journey that included sharks, starvation, enemy capture and inhuman brutality.

After the war, he returned home and got married to a dynamic young woman named Cynthia. But instead of celebrating his survival and marriage, he lost himself in alcohol and became obsessed with returning to Japan to murder his chief tormentor in the prison camp. His career and life collapsed, and soon—

even though they had a young daughter—Cynthia felt she had no choice but to arrange a divorce.

As they waited to handle all of the paperwork, Cynthia and Louie were walking down a hallway in their building one day when another couple mentioned that an evangelist named Billy Graham was preaching downtown. Cynthia was intrigued, and when Louie refused to take her to hear Graham speak, she went alone.

Upon returning home, she told Louie that she wasn't going to divorce him. What Louie saw as great news was followed by something he almost couldn't stomach: Cynthia said that she'd experienced a religious awakening. And she wanted Louie to go listen to Graham.

At first, Louie wouldn't hear of it. But Cynthia kept asking. Louie kept saying no—until, finally, he didn't.

That night, Louie sat down to listen to the young preacher and found himself slightly charmed. It didn't last. Louie wound up enraged by Graham's depiction of Judgment Day—and by Louie's own understanding of how God might view him, given his drinking and failure as a husband and father. He literally ran out of the tent, pulling Cynthia along with him.

The next day, Cynthia tried for hours to coax him into seeing Graham again. He refused. She refused to back down. They argued until, finally, Cynthia wore him down and Louie agreed to go, swearing he wouldn't stay until the end. This time, Graham asserted: "What God asks of men is belief. His invisibility is the truest test of that belief. To know who sees him, God makes himself unseen."

Struck by these words, Louie had a flashback. He remembered the incredible circumstances of his survival on the raft, and a promise he made to God while he was floating on it: "If you will save me, I will serve you forever." In that moment, he had asked for what he wanted in a spirit of complete and simple belief. Remembering the moment six years later had reignited that same belief in him now. What had he been thinking all these years? How could he have forgotten?

Hillenbrand writes: "It was the last flashback he would ever have. Louie let go of Cynthia and turned toward Graham. He felt supremely alive . . .

"Cynthia kept her eyes on Louie all the way home. When they entered the apartment, Louie went straight to his cache of liquor. It was the time of night when the need usually took hold of him, but for the first time in years, Louie had no desire to drink. He carried the bottles to the kitchen sink, opened them, and poured their contents into the drain. Then he hurried through the apartment, gathering packs of cigarettes, a secret stash of girlie magazines, everything that was part of his ruined years. He heaved it all down the trash chute."

Cynthia had effectively asked Louie to listen to Billy Graham's message of belief. When he decided to listen, it saved his marriage, his career, and his life.

Powerful Observations about Belief:

"And all things you ask in prayer, believing, you will receive."
    —Bible, Matthew 21:22

"A lot of companies have chosen to downsize, and maybe that was the right thing for them. We chose a different path. Our belief was that if we kept putting great products in front of customers, they would continue to open their wallets."
    —Steve Jobs, co-founder and CEO of Apple

"It's the repetition of affirmations that leads to belief. And once that belief becomes a deep conviction, things begin to happen."
—Muhammad Ali, world heavyweight champion boxer

"Belief in one's self is one of the most important bricks in building any successful venture."
—Lydia M. Child, American abolitionist, women's rights activist, Indian rights activist, novelist, and journalist

"Ask and it shall be given to you; seek and you shall find; knock and it shall be opened to you. For everyone who asks receives, and he who seeks finds, and to him who knocks, it shall be opened."
—Bible, Matthew 7:7-8

"All of the different religious faiths, despite their philosophical differences, have a similar objective. Every religion emphasizes a belief in human improvement, love, respect for others, sharing other people's suffering."
— His Holiness The 14th Dalai Lama, Tenzin Gyatso

"I have evidence of His direction, so many instances when I have been controlled by some other power than my own will that I cannot doubt His power."
—Abraham Lincoln, U.S. president

"I believe in one God, Creator of the Universe, that He governs it by His providence. That He ought to be worshiped. That the most acceptable service we render to Him is doing good to His other children. That the soul of man is immortal and will be treated with justice in another life respecting its conduct in this."
—Benjamin Franklin, writer, inventor and diplomat

"Yes, I believe in God."
—Last words of Columbine High School student Cassie Bernall

"Why, sometimes I believe as many as six impossible things before breakfast."
—Lewis Carroll, author

"We can believe what we choose. We are answerable for what we choose to believe."
—John Henry Newman, in a letter to Mrs. William Fraude

"If you have abandoned one faith, do not abandon all faith. There is always an alternative to the faith we lose. Or is it the same faith under a different mask?"
—Graham Greene, author

"I know in my heart that man is good. That what is right will eventually triumph. And there's purpose and worth to each and every life."
—Ronald Reagan, U.S. president

"You know that being an American is more than a matter of where your parents came from. It is a belief that all men are created free and equal and that everyone deserves an even break."
—Harry S. Truman, U.S. president

"I mean, as an athlete, as a competitor, you have to have that belief in yourself."
—Tiger Woods, golf champion

"The thing always happens that you really believe in; and the belief in a thing makes it happen."
—Frank Lloyd Wright, architect

"Create the highest, grandest vision possible for your life because you become what you believe."
—Oprah Winfrey, media magnate

The *ASK* Paradigm

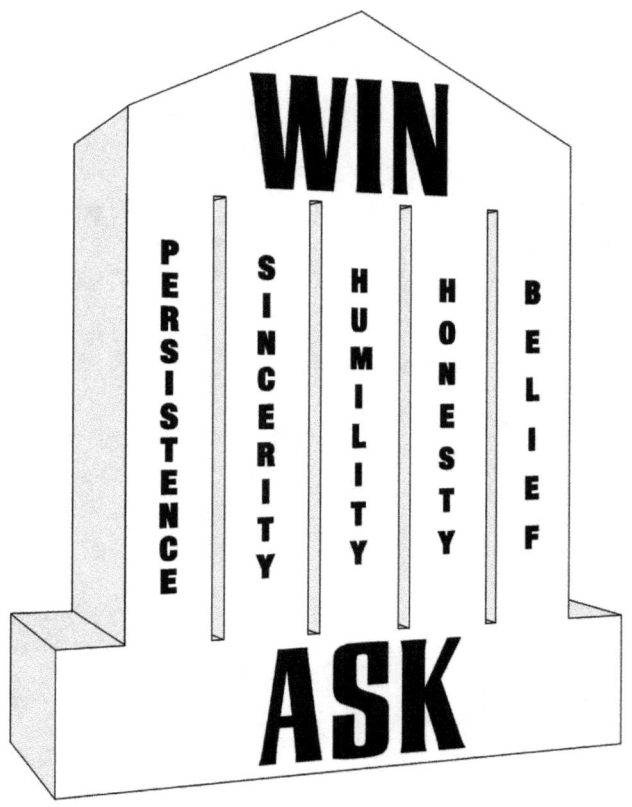

Think outside your comfort zone to fulfill wants using the 5 Win Words: Persistence, Sincerity, Humility, Honesty and Belief.

Part II

Ask for Wants

PLAN TO ASK

A bright, warming early morning sun does not just suddenly appear. Each morning, the full brilliance of morning occurs slowly as light gradually replaces darkness, and the world emerges from night, through dawn, into day. Similarly, asking effectively requires a slow evolution before the full sunburst of choices becomes apparent. The dawn is the planning process.

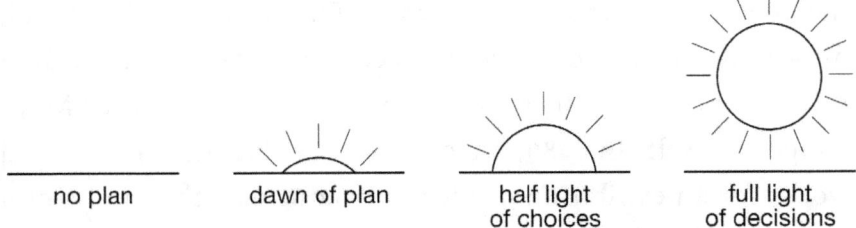

no plan   dawn of plan   half light of choices   full light of decisions

If you educate yourself on the issues, know the players, and set goals, the probability of fulfilling a want is high. Alternatively, ignorance of facts, denial of truths, and unclear intentions will produce a basket of frustrations.

I am an attorney and planner by profession. Every working day is committed to helping people improve future outcomes. I have found that planning works, both good and bad. Three stories illustrate. The first is famous in art history. The second and third are personal.

Picasso's Prophesy

Although Pablo Picasso was acclaimed as the towering genius of 20th-century art, his relationships with his wives, mistresses, and children were characterized by frustration, bitterness, refusal to negotiate conclusions, and an unwillingness to ask for or offer help. Picasso made a prophesy before his death: "When I die, it will be like a shipwreck, and as when a huge ship sinks, many people all around will be sucked down with it."

When Picasso died in 1973, it took five years of litigation to settle the estate. It was estimated that the legal fees equaled one of the shares—about one-tenth the value of his estate. The estate was valued for tax purposes at $260 million, and included almost 5,000 artistic works. On the day of his funeral, his grandson Pablito swallowed a container of bleach. He died three months later. In 1977, the mother of his daughter Maya hanged herself. In 1986, his second wife, Jacqueline, selected works for an exhibition of Picasso's paintings, then put a gun to her head and shot herself.

Picasso did have a calculated family plan—for chaos and destruction, which worked to perfection. His life and death proved that planning works—good or bad. The planned legacy he left through his art is priceless and timeless. His unwillingness to ask for help or offer help produced a titanic family disaster.

Abby's Loving Decision

The second story is about marital love, spontaneously told by clients as we sipped coffee in my office. Abby and Ken were referred to me for an intergenerational estate plan. Three children, ages 10, 12 and 16, were the motivation. Married 21 years, they were a two-income family, both working full time.

They asked for my professional help in designing a plan that would assure four years of debt-free college education for each of their three children under every circumstance. They expressed themselves openly. And they were a pleasure to work with.

In every first interview, I ask about family to better understand generational dynamics. In the course of highlighting important family matters, Abby spontaneously added their own romantic chronicle.

> We had been dating two years. While I thought our relationship was moving to a commitment, Ken did not see it that way. He wasn't sure he wanted to get married, to me or anyone else. Unexpectedly, I received a better job offer, which would require a move to another city. Ken thought a long-distance romance would work. I didn't.
>
> I asked my best friend what to do. Her eye-opening advice was, "Ask him to marry you!" I laughed. She reiterated, "I'm serious! If you love him, you need to force a decision. If he is never going to marry you, you need to know." In my heart, I knew my friend was right. Anxiously, I made a plan to ask.
>
> The next Sunday, I arranged an afternoon walk in the park with Ken. I rehearsed what I would say, realizing there were many ways to ask the same question. We sat down on a park bench next to a bed of blooming flowers under a maple tree. I posed a question with alternatives: "Ken, I want to be married

to you, but if you are not going to marry me, we should not see each other again."

Ken interrupted with a wide smile. "Best proposal I've ever received. Best decision I've ever made. Now, how can we help our children?" Instead of waiting passively for a proposal from Ken, Abby took the initiative and decided to ask for what she wanted. To ask effectively, she first made a plan—that is, she rehearsed how she would do it. And it worked brilliantly.

Big R Makes a Deal

The third story about "planning to ask" is about a business deal. Big R believes you must ask effectively to negotiate successfully. He illustrates with this story:

> As a seller, I was meeting with the representative of a prospective buyer of a developed and zoned site for a convenience store. My goal was to sell the property for the highest fair price.
>
> I planned the strategies for the negotiation session in advance. I invited the representative to my office. By meeting there, I had the advantage of familiarity and control of the surroundings. I asked four people to attend the meeting in addition to myself: an engineer, a friendly real estate agent, a note taker, and a person with a laptop computer. The engineer was to present quick answers to any technical questions. The agent was to cajole and reaffirm the fairness of our offer. The note taker had knowledge of the deal and experience in asking good questions. The computer person was a last-minute addition to give the appearance of importance to the meeting. I arranged the seating, with the representative sitting next to me.

I intentionally arrived 10 minutes late to the meeting, allowing time for small talk between the various people. After everyone was seated, I participated in the small talk for another five minutes. The talk was punctuated with laughter. Then I asked for the presentation by the representative and comments by others in the room. Staff came in with drinks and cookies.

I made sure all the representative's technical questions had answers. In the process of discussion, it became clear a great deal of time and expense had already been invested in the deal. Intentionally, the last topic was the purchase price. We were 55 minutes into our hour-long meeting. With so little time remaining, everyone was restless, ready to move on. I led off in a new direction on price.

"We can't accept your offer," I told her.

"We can't pay your asking price," she responded.

"That's what it's worth," I said.

"I can't sell that to my people in Texas."

"Then why did we do all this work?"

"Because we want the property."

"Okay, so write a check."

"I can't write a check, even if my client accepts your price."

"When can you?"

"If all goes as planned, in two to four months."

"Two to four months? We'll all go broke. Anyway, I'm going to Hawaii."

"When?"

"As soon as I can. If you will give me my money, we can both go to Hawaii."

"I'd like to leave here with a contract," she said.

"And we'd like to have a fair price. How about $_____?"

She thought a moment, then relented. She made a call to her client and discussed our counteroffer. When she hung up, she allowed herself a hint of a smile. "We're good to go," she said.

The meeting ended in one hour. We got our targeted price. The deal closed without a hitch.

As a counselor-at-law, I have listened to countless life stories. Many illustrate how asking effectively for wants can deliver happiness and bring momentous change to our lives.

ASK FOR MONEY

According to the experts, the No. 1 cause of divorce in this country isn't sex or religion or problems with the in-laws. It's fighting over money.

There are few things in a relationship that do more to solidify bonds and create a strong marriage than planning financial futures together. Think about it. Most couples decide to spend their lives together because they sincerely love each other and want to build a family unit. I've never met a couple who said, "Wouldn't it be great to live together so we can fight on a regular basis about our finances?" Even though no one wants to fight about money, the fact is that most couples do. Either that, or they flat-out avoid the subject.

If people fail to manage personal finances, they may suffer a financial crash followed by bankruptcy. I served as trustee in over 450 bankruptcy cases filed by people who could not see light at the end of their financial tunnel because it was filled with debts they could not pay. My job was to ask questions in search of assets to pay the bankrupt's creditors. In the process, I listened to each bankrupt's personal story of financial failure. I learned most failures were due to financial ignorance and poor planning.

If you want financial security, you must seek it. You need to take classes, read books, study the stock market, and make friends with financially successful people—that is, expand your circle of influence. You must ask others for help, but only after gaining the knowledge necessary to distinguish good advice from bad, reserving final decisions for your own informed judgment.

When someone offers you financial counsel, always consider the source: Is this person humble, honest, persistent, sincere, and faithful? He or she should demonstrate all of these personal character qualities before earning your confidence.

Bruce's SWAN Deals

Bruce attended college for only six weeks before dropping out and taking a routine clerical position in the home office of a natural gas company in southeastern Colorado. Frustrated with the boredom of organizing the daily reports that came across his desk, he quit that job and moved to Denver. There, he tried marketing life insurance. He discovered he was a good salesman. He liked listening to other people's stories and telling a few of his own. He threw himself into selling with a passion.

After a year in the business, Bruce was finally beginning to enjoy the fruits of his hard work when his older brother, Bud, called. Bruce tells his story.

"Do you think you could sell houses?" Bud asked me.

"I won't know until I try," I replied. That simple conversation was the beginning of a family partnership that made us both multimillionaires.

Mostly, we did it with what we call SWAN deals. It stands for "Start Without A Nickel," and it means exactly that. Start with nothing. When my brother, Bud, called all those years ago, he needed help with a SWAN deal. He owned a small construction company that had just purchased a large piece of land for a new housing development. The deal was seller-financed, which means Bud's company did not put any money into the deal but owed a ton to the seller, which was due in installments.

The risk was high. A lot of houses would have to be built and sold quickly to generate cash flow. Bud's company signed the promissory note, which avoided personal liability. If the project tanked, he would lose the company, but not his personal savings. His problem was that he knew how to build houses, but had no idea how to sell them. That would be my role, if I was interested.

I was very interested. It sounded to me like a great opportunity. My wife was on board because we could live in one of the project houses with our three daughters. Times were good. Dumb luck was on our side. We sold every house. In fact, we pre-sold most of them before any dirt was moved. We paid off the debt on the land, and within three years, we were ready to roll into the next SWAN deal.

At the time we talked, the construction industry was trying to dig out of a recession. So I observed that it must be a lot tougher than it used to be to find that kind of deal. Bruce continued:

> We're doing a different kind of SWAN deal these days. We've enjoyed our share of success, and we figured it was time to give something back. To do that, we started a scholarship fund we call Reach Your Peak to help financially disadvantaged college kids make it through.
>
> We've given scholarships to 248 deserving young people so far. Anne and I invite wealthy donors and college students

in need over to our house for a free dinner. The kids tell the donors their stories—some of them bring us to tears. Afterward, we send out a follow-up letter asking for scholarship donations. The checks come in every time. It's not rocket science. It's just another SWAN deal.

Bruce is a salesman, always asking others. The rewards have satisfied his wants, first by filling his pockets, then by helping others.

Martha's 10 Percent

An elderly widow came to my office to discuss how she might transfer her wealth to her children and grandchildren. Martha and her husband had built up a sizable estate over the years, despite earning only modest incomes in the U.S. Postal Service. I asked how they had managed to do it. She told me a story:

> Neither of us came from money, and we didn't have college educations. We lived in St. Louis, Missouri, in those days, and we were struggling to keep our heads above water. But we made a decision that transformed all our lives, shortly after our marriage.
> One day, we realized we were tired of living hand to mouth, always struggling just to make ends meet. So we decided to become rich. The first step, we thought, would be to build up a small nest egg.
> Together, we started putting 10 percent of our paychecks each week into a special savings account we had opened for just that purpose. After a few months, we went to a local stockbroker's office to open an account. We began to invest, and continued to save.

Of course, things didn't always go smoothly. Initially, we bought four stocks, and they all went to zero in less than a year. But we kept trying. We realized the problem was not the stock market or the stockbroker or even the particular stocks we had chosen. The problem was us. We didn't know the first thing about finance. We had never taken a class on investing. It was the blind leading the blind. We decided to seek help.

We realized if we were going to get rich, we had to learn how to get rich. You have to learn to earn. We read, took classes, listened to people selling products or services, talked to friends. We asked questions. Finally, when we decided we knew enough to make decisions, we did so. And when we decided we knew enough to change those decisions, we did.

We never did become rich. But we always had enough to satisfy our needs and most of our desires, and even enough to help other people in need.

Today, anyone can become an investor. With so many brokerage houses online, it's never been easier to get started. But becoming an investor and becoming financially secure are not the same thing. You need to constantly seek new knowledge about money management to avoid ending up like 90 percent of all Americans, struggling to survive during retirement. Always seek new knowledge. Ask for help. Then actively manage your personal finances.

ASK FOR LOVE

Beth Tries Online Dating

"Love is out there. We can help you find it." With that intriguing invitation, eHarmony.com invites people to join the online dating service for a fee.

The service claims it has over 33 million users, and that on average, 542 people get married every day in the United States because of eHarmony—accounting for almost 5 percent of new U.S. marriages. Participants begin by completing a relationship questionnaire, which is used in the matching system.

Beth is a believer. She has been teaching third grade in a rural Colorado school for years. Her time in the classroom with the kids was gratifying, but lonely evenings and weekends seemed getting longer and longer. All of the single teachers at her school were women. She did not do the bar scene, and was not meeting any eligible singles at the large church she attended.

With quiet embarrassment, she logged onto eHarmony, filled in the information, and pressed the Enter key. She told no one of her new online effort to expand her social life.

Almost immediately, she received the personality profiles of several single men. She decided to open communication with a guy named Dan, a former schoolteacher who was in the middle of a career change—a move she was also considering. He was now a third-year student in law school. Following eHarmony's protocol, they wrote introductory letters to each other. Beth explains how virtual reality became a fast-track romance:

> From our online communications, I realized that our goals and faith were perfectly matched. The age differential was comfortable. He had a way of expressing himself with words that made me smile. We decided to meet in Castle Rock for lunch on a Saturday, halfway between our locations. We hit it off from the beginning—no surprises, no disappointments. We both enthusiastically decided to meet again.
>
> We exchanged letters, which we both saved, and are now treasures. My lonely weekends were replaced with romance and an entirely new social scene. We became engaged, with marriage plans after he finished law school and passed the bar examination. I finished my year of teaching. Time flashed by. We have now been married 18 months. Each month is better than the last.

By logging on to an Internet dating service, Beth asked effectively for help to fulfill the emptiness in her life with a loving partner. She stopped procrastinating, took the initiative, and tried a new way to fulfill her wants. And she hit a jackpot!

Leigh's Fear of Love

The following story played out among people I know quite well: a young woman, the man she loves, and a struggling mother. Perhaps what is most interesting about the narrative is that each had to ask for something from the other in order for the relationships among them to work. The young woman, Leigh, told it this way:

> Wayne and I were enjoying a hot summer evening, sipping cool drinks at a sidewalk café. Our relationship had been simmering ever since we met in a summer school class a year before. Several previous times, Wayne tried to talk with me about the future of our relationship. He said he loved me. I always stopped the conversation. Finally, he asked the inevitable question: "Why is this so difficult for you to talk about? Don't you love me too?"
>
> "It's not that," I said, suddenly and inexplicably on the verge of tears.
>
> "What is it, then? Are you afraid of loving someone?"
> That startled me. Wayne waited silently for a reply. I struggled to find an answer. "Maybe," I murmured.
>
> "Why are you afraid?" he asked. "I'd like to be able to talk about this, Leigh, so we can move forward in our relationship."
>
> Again I was silent. I was afraid of the answer, though to be honest, I did know what it was. After a few moments, I took a deep breath and began to tell him a story.
>
> "When I was seventeen," I said, "I was failing in school. I stayed out late at night, ran around with the wrong crowd, and attended parties where drugs were used. Mother and I lived together. My father had deserted us when I was 3 years old. Alcoholism controlled his life. He ended up committing suicide in a lonely hotel room. Mother then began devoting herself to preparing me for the dangers I would face in life, especially from men.
>
> "She also tried to form a close bond with me, but I didn't

cooperate. She always complained I wouldn't open up to her, wouldn't talk about my problems or discuss my feelings. She would say, 'I know I must have faults, too. If you tell me about my faults, I will do everything I can to correct them.'

"One day, I finally decided to try to open up. We were in the car. She was driving. I said, 'Mother, I need to tell you something important. I haven't talked to you about this before because I was afraid to hurt you, but you say you want me to be honest, so here goes. Mother, I love you, but I'm also angry with you. Terribly angry. I don't know all the reasons for my feelings. I think they have a lot to do with you always saying bad things about my Dad—and about all other men, too. I feel that no matter what Dad did, he was still my father, and you have no right to drag him down—especially since he's not here to tell his side of the story. Because of what happened between you and him, you've tried to make me fear, hate, and despise all men. And I need to ask you to stop doing that.'

"Mother flew into a horrible rage and screamed, 'How dare you! You don't know what that man put me through! You have no idea what my life has been like. I've done everything for you, and your father did nothing. Apparently, you have never understood anything I've said about him.'

"The next day, mother quieted down considerably. When I reminded her of what she had said, she asked me earnestly to forgive her. She realized she'd bungled an opportunity to discuss relationships with me. She entered psychotherapy to work on her part of our problem.

"Good things have happened for my mother following our discussion about Dad. For one thing, she's stopped beating up on him. In fact, she never mentions him anymore.

What's more, her attitude about men has gone from negative to positive. She's engaged to be married."

After I finished my story, I looked directly into Wayne's blue eyes, reached for his hand, and smiled. "Wayne, I'm glad you asked. I've never discussed this with anyone else. And yes, I may be afraid of loving someone, but I'm willing to try. I like being with you very much."

ASK FOR OPPORTUNITY

Tanya Was a Rebel

Sometimes our first lesson in asking comes in the form of someone else asking something of us. That happened to Tanya many years before she became my client. She was a high school student with a real attitude problem. In her own words:

> I was a rebel without a cause. By the end of my sophomore year, I had dyed my hair a shade of blue, worked a few hours a week in a counter-culture youth clothing store, and had a 1.8 grade point average. Hanging around with other underachievers did not help my attitude. The school counselor warned I was up for academic probation and suggested I attend a community college for remedial work before continuing high school.
>
> At the time, my parents were divorced and struggling with their own personal and financial challenges. The only person who seemed interested in my state of mind was my history teacher. When I did not turn in a homework assignment one day, he asked me to stay after class. Instead of the usual

put-downs most teachers gave me, he asked why I was not using my God-given talents. He believed I had an aptitude for history and could become one of his best students, if I made a commitment. Then he posed a challenging question. "Will you make a commitment to become one of my best students?"

To please him and to squirm out of an increasingly uncomfortable conversation, I replied, "Yes." Looking directly at me without a blink, he challenged me again. "Do you mean it?"

I reaffirmed with another "Yes."

I did take those community college remedial courses to improve my study skills, and I repeated two high school courses in summer school. I graduated with a 3.6 grade point average my senior year, with honors in history and a determination to someday help other kids who were struggling the way I had been.

University admission was easier than tuition financing. The family cupboard was bare. My scholarship application was denied with a form letter, stamped with the name of a student aid officer. Sometimes, when you ask for help, you get no for an answer. That wasn't an answer I was willing to accept.

I called the student aid office and advised I was appealing the denial. The secretary said there was no appeal process, the decision was final, but I could talk to a staff person. The next day I met with the financial aid officer and her assistant. I told them my story, including my goal of helping others who are struggling through high school. After a 15-minute conversation, they excused themselves briefly, then returned and offered me a half scholarship plus a work-study program to pay all costs for my first year. With good grades, I could renew the financial package for four years. With a Cheshire cat grin and a pumping handshake, I accepted.

True to my goals, after graduation, I applied for a position with a worldwide kids' leadership program. The purpose of the program was to build academic, social, and personal success skills. Six years into my career, I still wear that Cheshire cat grin.

Tanya's history teacher helped her get off the road to nowhere by asking her to change direction and head toward a worthy goal. Once Tanya got her redirected momentum going, she used that same technique—asking effectively—to take her to new destinations.

Rob's Disability Becomes an Opportunity

Big R's son, Rob, has cerebral palsy. Multiple surgeries have given his legs partial mobility, but he can cover only short distances at a time, and he must use a walker. Most of the time, a wheelchair takes him where he needs to go. As a boy, he struggled through public schools with the loving support of his mother, a former schoolteacher, and two older brothers, who were often Rob's stand-ins for healthy arms and legs.

Big R was proud of his family. He knew that their positive adjustments to his son's handicaps were critical not only to Rob's future welfare, but to that of everyone else in the household as well. Rob needed to be loved and accepted as he was, with all of his disabilities, whatever they might be. And he required exactly the same kind of love his brothers received. He needed emotional support, but not smothering; care, but not overindulgence; and opportunities for achievement, self-control, and social growth toward an independent place in society.

Now an adult, Rob has discovered that although his handicap has challenged him in some ways, in other ways it has given him unique opportunities. As a teenager, he loved to listen to music and longed to be a radio disc jockey, but his disabilities proved too severe for that career track. Instead, he made a special effort to meet the people who wrote and sang the songs he loved.

He asked for permission to go to recording sessions and watch. The artists were more than glad to respond. They began inviting Rob to their sessions on a regular basis. Here's how Rob told the rest of his story a few years ago.

> I learned as much as possible about the recording industry. Then I began to ask undiscovered new writers, composers, and artists if they would let me represent them as their agent. Some said yes. I matched my new clients with small recording labels and helped them cut their first records. More recordings followed.
>
> After a while, I created my own publishing company and recording label. My agency currently holds the rights to over 500 new songs. I have released CDs that have been on the Grammy Entry List in 39 separate categories, including Album of the Year, Rock Album of the Year, Pop Album of the Year, Country Album of the Year, and Song of the Year. Television series use my music in their programming. Radio jockeys are selecting my record label. Retail sales are going up.
>
> I attend the Grammy Awards, and I am invited to speak at conventions worldwide. My handicap actually works in my favor—it attracts media attention to my record label and my artists. My picture often appears with famous singers and politicians. I'm becoming a celebrity!

In the beginning, Rob had asked for help from others. Now, others ask for help from him. Wants are being fulfilled.

ASK FOR JOBS

Karl Was Afraid of Failing

Karl's family was growing faster than his income. With a wife, two young children, and a baby due in five months, he knew it was time to look for another place to live. Their two-bedroom apartment just wouldn't be big enough.

His undergraduate degree in business helped him get an entry-level job in the healthcare industry, supervising accounts receivable for a group medical practice. He was responsible for filling all patient insurance claims, Medicare and Medicaid payments, and collecting overdue accounts. Occasionally, he had to turn large delinquencies over to a collection agency to file suit, obtain a court judgment, and garnish a patient's wages. He hated that part of the job. What he hated even more was that the position offered no opportunity for advancement. He felt his career was going nowhere.

His wife, Kate, soon noticed how discontented he was. "What do you really think you would be good at?" she asked him one Saturday morning over coffee.

"Selling," Karl blurted, almost instinctively. "I'm a good

communicator. As a salesman, I could work my own hours, and I'd be willing to put in a lot more of them than I do now."

"So?" his wife said. "Why don't you try selling?"

"I'm afraid of failing. We need more money, and I don't think I'd make much for a while. And I would need some training before I even faced my first customer."

"What could you sell?"

"Real estate," he said without hesitation. "I've always been fascinated with real estate. My aunt was a successful real estate agent. She made enough to put two children through college and to take cruises all around the world."

"I think you should try it!" Kate challenged.

He thought about it for a moment. "Suppose it doesn't work out," he said.

"It will," she replied. "I have faith in you."

On Saturday, Karl called a local real estate company owner, Frank, with whom he had an acquaintance. A few months before, they had worked together on a community fundraising drive to help underprivileged kids go to summer camp. Together, they had exceeded their fundraising goals by 50 percent.

After some small talk, Karl plucked up his courage and blurted out the reason for his call: "I want to work for you, Frank. I want to become a real estate agent. I'll be the best agent you ever hired."

"I'm glad to hear that," Frank replied. "I've seen how you work with people, and I think you're right—you'd make a good salesman. Maybe great. When can you start?"

Karl and Kate agreed on a plan. Karl would take night and weekend courses to earn his real estate sales license, then move full-time into his new career.

The rest, as they say, is history. Karl's commission income exceeded his old salary within six months. A year later, he was making twice what he had earned at his previous job. He and his wife bought a house from a bank foreclosure. He used his new network of contacts to obtain a favorable mortgage. Buyers and sellers began to ask for his help.

Karl then stepped up to the challenge of the commercial real estate market. He and a partner bought a troubled income property and filled it with new tenants drawn from his business network. Rental income has given him the freedom to travel, spend time with children and grandchildren, and volunteer to raise money to send more kids to summer camp.

Cathy Was Assigned to the 'Dumb Class'

Cathy took a unique route in search of a career opportunity, and she found what she was looking for.

> Things were tough for me at school. I really thought that I would never amount to anything. From the day I started first grade, I could not keep up, and I knew that I was not going to be a successful student. By the time I was in high school, I was assigned to the "dumb class." However, I did find one subject I liked and did well in. Electronics shop was interesting and fun. I have a knack for fixing things. And there were very few girls in the class.
>
> When my teacher asked me what I wanted to do, I told her I wanted to be a waitress—in other words, I had no ambition to do anything. At 16, I dropped out of school.
>
> By the time I was 20, I was carrying credit card and loan debt of around $20,000, due to my complete ignorance about money. By 25, I was a single mother on welfare, living in a rented space with a friend. I spent my time trying to get more

money out of the government instead of trying to create my own income.

But to qualify for government benefits, I had to take some classes at a community college to re-enter the work force. I had no idea where to start. I needed help, so I asked for it—I made an appointment to speak with a career counselor at the college. She gave me a bunch of aptitude tests, and an IQ test, I think, and interviewed me for about an hour. Then she made some recommendations.

Her advice led me to sign up for two courses that changed my life. The first was in electronics repair, the second in business finance.

The business finance course opened my eyes. For the first time in my life, I saw the connection between money management, career, and success. I needed to set a better example for my son, Kevin, than I had done so far. I became a dedicated student and earned an A in both classes.

Using my knowledge and experience in fixing electronic devices, I got a low-level job going to people's homes on telephone service calls. For the first time in my life, I enjoyed going to work. And I was good at solving problems, from cut lines to new equipment installation. If I didn't know the answer, I researched it until I did.

I also found out that the telephone company I worked for subcontracted work to outside vendors. I decided to explore that possibility. Lessons learned from my business finance class helped me create a rudimentary business plan. I could make more money subcontracting jobs than I could as an employee of the telephone company. And eventually, I could have people working for me. I asked for a meeting with a manager in service and repair.

The interview was scary. I told him about my training and experience, and I described my goals as a young, single parent. And then I asked earnestly for a chance to prove I could be their best subcontractor. I became a little choked up and teary.

Within a year, I had a subcontracting agreement with the telephone company and one employee working for me. In two years, I had three employees working for me. Within three years, I had five employees doing the job, I was running the business full-time from my home, and I was able to spend quality time with Kevin.

I now use only one credit card, and I pay the balance off every month. Also, I still take courses on electronics repair and money management. I feel you can never have too much education. If projections hold, I will have 10 employees next year and qualify for a small business loan to purchase an office warehouse building.

ASK FOR HEALTH

Lew Almost Waits Too Long

Lew is a longtime friend. A university professor with a Ph.D. in economics, he is revered by his students, and he's one smart dude. But his unwillingness to ask for help almost cost him his life.

During our monthly social breakfast, he complained of pain in his abdomen that he'd had for several days. He thought it was just an upset stomach, took some over-the-counter medication, and anxiously waited for the discomfort to disappear. Two days later, still experiencing no relief, he went to see his family doctor, who diagnosed a gallstone. A subsequent ultrasound confirmed the diagnosis, but unknown to him at the time, missed the accompanying infection. He was told to see a specialist. When he called for an appointment, he was told the first available time would be in two weeks.

Lew lived alone. I called a few days later to check up on his condition. He did not answer the phone but returned the call later.

"Lew, this has been going on for a week. I'll drive you to the hospital emergency room. You need immediate treatment," I told him.

"I'll be okay. I have a doctor's appointment in a week," he replied meekly.

We repeated this conversation on each of the next three days, always with a return call hours after my call to him. During each conversation, Lew sounded weaker, complaining of constant pain and no sleep.

In frustration and desperation, I called Milt, a medical doctor friend, and asked a favor. Would he make a house call? He agreed to visit Lew that evening. I left a message with Lew's answering service, hoping he would open the door when the doctor rang the doorbell, which he did. After a quick professional medical evaluation, Lew was taken to the hospital for emergency surgery to remove his gallbladder and begin draining and treating the abdominal infection that had by now become life-threatening.

The surgeon opined, "If the infection had been allowed to continue two more days, it would have been irreversibly terminal." As it was, Lew endured major surgery, 10 days in the hospital, and 45 days recovering at home. Treated early, it would have required a one-hour outpatient visit.

Lew is a brilliant professor, but his unwillingness to ask for help almost cost him his life. If he would have asked effectively for help at the first sign of a problem, or later accepted the volunteer help that his friends had offered, he would have been a much happier camper in life's ever-changing campground.

John Asks to Die in Peace

A few months before his heart attack, John watched the slow, agonizing death of his wife, who had suffered brain damage after resuscitation from her own heart attack. He resolved that nothing like that would ever happen to him. When his time came, he told his children they should simply let him die. He told his doctors the same thing.

John was visiting friends at a Chicago center for the elderly when he felt chest pains and collapsed. In the hospital's coronary care unit, he told his doctor that, should his condition worsen, he did not want to be resuscitated. John gave the same instructions to his three daughters. His doctor entered those instructions on John's chart, but the instructions were not recorded on the monitor by his bed. Thus, three days later, when he began experiencing ventricular fibrillations that signaled sudden death, a nurse applied electrodes to his chest and revived him.

John would probably have died from the heart attack if the nurse had not intervened. In some ways, his case is a miracle of modern medicine. Yet it was not the fate John or his family wanted, since two days after he was revived, he suffered a debilitating stroke. John's medical bills spiraled to over $250,000, depleting his life savings before life support was discontinued.

His daughters observed, "Dad wanted to die in peace. He was a pretty staunch Catholic and would never have taken his own life, but he didn't believe in dragging people back from the brink when their time had clearly come. He asked everybody to follow his instructions, his medical directives. Why didn't they?"

From my experience as a counselor-at-law, you must ask healthcare providers to follow your instructions and realize that asking once is rarely enough. Ask again. And then again. Your loved ones may need to ask for you, too. Keep asking until you're sure your thoughts have been heard by everyone who needs to hear them. Healthcare has become a very impersonal arena. If you do not ask for what you want, you will not get it.

ASK FOR JUSTICE

During my short career as a criminal defense attorney, the first five years out of law school, I was appointed by trial court judges to represent indigent criminal defendants. This happened when the public defenders were not available. Compensation was little or nothing. My greatest reward was learning how to ask effectively.

My job was to ask questions of prospective witnesses in and out of court to develop a defense to the criminal charges. "Where were you when the crime was committed?" "Who was with you?" "Are you telling me the truth?" "Will you testify on the witness stand under oath to tell the truth, the whole truth, and nothing but the truth?" "Will you tell the same story you have told me?"

I always tried to out-prepare the prosecuting attorney without regard to hours worked. I asked questions of prospective jurors during jury selection in an effort to identify open-minded people. I asked questions of the prosecution's witnesses in an effort to create reasonable doubts in the minds of the jurors. Attorneys asking effectively in court often prove the difference between guilty and not guilty jury verdicts, between a long jail sentence, even execution, and walking out of the courtroom free.

In my brief criminal defense attorney time, I represented defendants in nine separate jury trials, in federal and state trial courts. All my clients walked out of the courtroom free. Nine times, juries found my clients not guilty. It was not brilliance or Clarence Darrow oratory. Asking questions effectively made all the difference.

The following stories illustrate justice-related experiences you might encounter. Always consider asking for help.

The Cop Forgives Me

Powder snow, blue sky, no wind, moderate temperatures—a perfect ski day, I reflected, looking one last time at the snow-capped 14,000-foot peaks as I shouldered my skis at day's end. Once or twice a year, I reserve some solo time for myself, when I can have some outdoor fun and independent thoughts.

As I headed for home, paralleling the beautiful Arkansas River, I tuned the radio to the Denver Broncos football game. They were playing their nemesis, the Oakland Raiders. The score was tied, with five minutes left in the game, and the Broncos had the ball. "Could they, would they, can they?" I wondered.

The announcer's excitement was captivating. He kept my attention riveted to every play—until I saw red and blue lights flashing in my rearview mirror. So much for my perfect day. I pulled over to the side of the highway, with the state patrolman close behind. He exited his cruiser, leaving the lights flashing, and walked to my open window.

"You were traveling 80 miles an hour in a 60-mile-per-hour zone," he stated flatly.

"I was? I was not watching my speedometer."

"It's on the radar gun," he said. "A lot of folks speed in this section of the highway."

I tried to continue the conversation, simultaneously asking myself why I had been speeding. Suddenly it hit me. "Officer, are you listening to the Bronco football game?" I blurted. "It's tied with four minutes left, and the Broncos have the ball. Are you a fan?"

"Hmm. Forgot the game was on. Yeah, I follow them," he commented.

"Officer, I was so caught up in the game, I was not watching my speed. I apologize if I was traveling over the limit. It was unintentional. I'm an emotional Bronco fan. I'm coming home from a perfect day of skiing. Please don't spoil it by giving a speeding ticket. A warning is all I need today."

I felt like a child hoping for some sign of forgiveness from a parent. The patrolman shifted his weight to one foot. The corners of his mouth turned up ever so slightly. After a bit more conversation, the officer made a decision. "Okay, no ticket this time, but drive carefully. Keep the speed down. There's another state trooper up the road."

"Thank you," I said appreciatively.

He walked back to his cruiser, turned off the flashing lights, and maybe turned on the last minute of the game—which, unfortunately, the Broncos lost.

In return for an honest, humble acknowledgment of a mistake, I was able to avoid a negative outcome.

My law practice includes daily dealings with police officers, prosecuting attorneys, witnesses, judges, lawyers, anyone who will listen. I plead for favorable outcomes for my clients. In the practice of law, there are attorneys who know how to ask and those who don't.

Steve's Inheritance is Hijacked

Intergenerational family inheritances are exploding into family feuds and courtroom battles. In recent years, legal estate hijacking has become a risk-and-reward game of chance. In many families, unintended beneficiaries are walking away with family inheritances—everything from dishes, pictures, and jewelry to homes and investments. I am reminded of a case that played out in my office, as Steve described the disappearance of his uncle's estate.

> Uncle Mark had no children of his own. He did, however, have one niece and one nephew: my sister and me.
>
> He and I had a special relationship. He taught me how to fish. We spent a lot of time together in his boat. I remember many good times when he picked me up before daybreak to be out on the lake when the fish began feeding. One time, we sat through a cold rain just to see who could catch the most fish. We laughed and shivered until Uncle Mark conceded defeat. I caught six bass and four bluegill; he caught four bass and five bluegill. Bass counted two points, bluegill one point. Final score: Uncle Mark 13, me 16. I still have the score written on the back of a fishhook package.
>
> Uncle Mark told me he intended to make a will. He was going to take care of his wife, Doris, for life and then give everything else to my sister and me. Uncle Mark owned commercial real estate and a beautiful home. He would have to go to an attorney for help, of course, but he didn't seem happy about that. For some reason I never quite understood, he had always shied away from working with lawyers.
>
> One morning, he went jogging on his customary route. About an hour later, a neighbor called his wife, Doris, to say Mark had been found lying beside a park path.

Someone called 911. Emergency vehicles arrived and sped him to a hospital, but he was already gone. He'd suffered a massive heart attack. He probably passed away instantly.

We soon learned he never wrote the will he'd talked about. So state law controlled, deciding who would administer the estate and who would receive the inheritance. In Uncle Mark's case, Doris got everything. She was appointed to administer the estate, and she received all of his property.

Our family hired a lawyer. She said there was nothing to do. State probate law was not on our side. Doris was in total control, smart, and protective. She had never related to our family. While Uncle Mark was alive, we saw her occasionally at a holiday family event. The 10-year marriage seemed to be based on travel companionship. She declined all family invitations after Uncle Mark's death.

Doris had been married once before, with one son. She was older than Uncle Mark. She smoked and enjoyed her afternoon cocktails. She died of cancer about two years after Mark's death. Our family lawyer pieced together the rest of the story.

When Doris died, she gave everything to her son. Apparently he was never able to hold a job, maybe because he did not manage his diabetes or, more likely, because of his drinking. He was divorced with three children. His ex-wife was constantly after him for delinquent child support. He moved around, supposedly looking for work, always staying one step ahead of the child support authorities.

Then events became bizarre. Doris' son was found dead in his van on a dirt road in the Arizona desert. We're not sure of the cause. His three children, from whom he had been hiding for several years, inherited all of Uncle Mark's property. Crazy!

A sad family outcome for Uncle Mark and those he loved. My memories are about what he said he was going to do and what he didn't do. I feel angry and sad. I try to forget, but I can't.

Planning doesn't happen by default. Don't rely on the law to receive the benefits or outcomes you expect or deserve. Planning requires asking effectively, and with timeliness, for help. Uncle Mark didn't ask.

LIST YOUR WANTS

Over and over again, clients have shown me that we all share the same basic needs, desires, and wants. Some are necessities: money, love, opportunity, health, and justice. Some simply serve to make life more enjoyable or satisfying: prestige, leisure time, achievement, travel.

To some people, wants are highly personal. "I want to say I'm sorry, fall in love, have children, connect with an old friend, exercise, have sex, pay off a credit card debt, learn a new skill, change jobs, move to another city, stop smoking, buy a high definition television, run a 10k, ride a motorcycle, live in a house so big you need a staff to clean it, marry a millionaire . . ."

For others, wants may be more group-oriented. "I want to go out to dinner with friends, go shopping with family, attend a reunion, start a new business, research genealogy, join a social club, attend church or other faith-based events, go to a movie and eat popcorn, take a cruise, visit a zoo . . ."

What would be on your list? Think about it. Consider the possibilities while lying in bed, driving, staring into space, sipping a cup of coffee. Ponder them when you're alone or when you're talking with a friend or a loved one. Your wants can be simple and comfortable, or outrageous and out-of-the-box. It doesn't matter. You can change them whenever you like.

Then, when you're clear about what you want, ask. There are many ways to do this. Announce your wants to the world. Or ask quietly, through silent prayer and meditation. People with disabilities must often ask for help, but they don't always verbalize their requests. Simply allowing others to see their challenges—blindness, deafness, debilitating injury—can be a very effective way to get what they need.

If you don't ask at all, however, there's a strong chance that your wants will remain frustratingly unfulfilled. As Natalie Johnson, a Colorado bookstore owner, elaborated, "I love the title page of this book because it will encourage all my frustrated friends to ask for what they want, instead of suffering in silence." People struggling with stress, frustration, depression, or fear are often unable to express their wants. And they often go without satisfying them.

Do you avoid asking others for help? If you do, here's a rule to remember: You will not get what you deserve. You will get what you negotiate. When you ask effectively for help, you are negotiating—and that's how you fulfill your wants. Far better things come to those who ask.

So what do you want? It's time to make your personal list. And don't just make it a pie-in-the-sky, abstract wish list. Give yourself deadlines. Where do you want to be, with regard to your wants, in a week, a month, and a year? Note your progress at the end of each time period. Check off the wants you've fulfilled. Here are some blank lists to help you get started.

List five wants to fill next week.

1. _____
2. _____

3. _____
4. _____
5. _____

List five wants to fill next month.

1. _____
2. _____
3. _____
4. _____
5. _____

List five wants to fill next year.

1. _____
2. _____
3. _____
4. _____
5. _____

SPOTLIGHT YOUR WANTS

Whatever seems out of control or out of reach today may be conquerable or within your grasp tomorrow, if you spotlight what you want. Spotlighting is making a commitment to focus your mind and body on one specific want—like focusing an unwavering high-energy light beam at one spot on the wall. With this technique, you can make seemingly unattainable wants into reality.

Two stories, poles apart, illustrate. The first, a cry for help to conquer marijuana addiction. The second, a desire to leave a legacy. Both spotlight asking for help to secure wants.

Tony Cries for Help

CHINS is an acronym for "Children in Need of Supervision," legally defined as children under age 18 who are out of control or a threat to themselves or others. These teenagers are usually runaways, using drugs, or threatening suicide or homicide.

As a county attorney for two years, I filed over 200 petitions on behalf of the state, asking a juvenile judge to find a teenager a CHINS. As I investigated and read reports about these children, I concluded the dominant factor was alcohol or drug use, or both, by the children or people influencing the child, including parents, relatives, friends, and people selling drugs. Marijuana was the overwhelming starter drug of choice.

This observation is increasingly important as more states approve laws legalizing the possession and use of medical and recreational marijuana in spite of federal laws making it illegal. Consider Tony's story:

> My mother and father split when I was in eighth grade. I started to struggle socially. My sports skills did not measure up to high school standards. I always felt slow and awkward, so it was no surprise. Girls liked the jocks.
>
> I started hanging out with a group of guys and girls who liked to meet after school and hang out together at a nearby park. They were unconditionally accepting. Asked me to join them. I liked their laid-back attitude about school. "Don't sweat the jocks. Take it easy. Don't take books home. Do homework during class."
>
> One warm afternoon, a girl offered me a smoke. I liked her. I thought she liked me. I knew it was pot. I wanted to be liked, to be accepted, to be a part of my new group. I shared the joint with her. This evolved into an after-school ritual. I became a pothead.
>
> An older kid and I got high one afternoon. He was driving his mother's car. Speeding too fast, we ran a stop sign. Terrible accident. A 7-year-old girl in the other car was killed. The driver of the car I was in was charged with vehicular homicide. I was a minor. The court declared I was a Child in Need of Supervision.
>
> After graduating from high school, I tried college for a

semester. By then, my pot use was costing me more than I could afford. I dropped out of college with D's and F's.

Finally, I hit bottom. I knew I had to ask for help. I called the social worker appointed to work with me in my CHINS case. I literally cried for help. She told me to go to the Internet and log on to Marijuana Anonymous. On the Internet, I found help. I found there was an organization waiting to help me. I concluded I was a marijuana addict, and could not manage my life without outside help. I read "The Twelve Steps of Marijuana Anonymous." The message encouraged me to attend meetings in person, online or by telephone. Meeting locations and telephone numbers were included.

With trepidation, I attended a Marijuana Anonymous (MA) meeting. My stress level was off the charts. During the meeting, I agreed to attend another meeting the following week. Slowly, I learned drug addiction is a lifelong disease requiring unfaltering management to prevent relapses. I made a commitment to conquer my addiction. I accepted the fact I need to ask for help. I have been drug-free for 10 months. I am going back to college. I am going to succeed this time.

Liesl Leaves a Legacy

Liesl's story also exemplifies spotlighting a want—a desire to leave a legacy. She discovered that by focusing her mind and energy she could simultaneously achieve a personal goal and inspire others.

Liesl believed passionately in education. With no children of her own, she volunteered her services at a local community college, helping students find housing or jobs, answering phones, assembling mailings, issuing parking permits, listening to complaints.

"I believe education is the most valuable asset we can acquire during our lifetime on this planet," she explains. "It is available to everyone, but it can't be bought, sold, or inherited. It can only be acquired by hard work. The knowledge it renders is available day and night, 365 days a year, and you can share it with others."

Liesl remained at the college for over 20 years. Three times, she received Volunteer of the Year recognition with her name on a plaque.

She dreamed of leaving a lasting legacy, a message to future generations of students, but she wasn't quite sure how to do it. She pondered the idea for several years. Her thoughts repeatedly returned to an old tower on the college grounds, a relic of an earlier era when the campus was a health recovery center. It seemed to her that the tower would be a perfect location for chimes. Liesl played in the hand bell choir at church. She loved the melodious sounds the hand bells produced.

Liesl shared her idea with campus administrators, faculty, staff, and students. "If the tower had electric chimes similar to my church's hand bells," she said to them enthusiastically, "the sounds could be heard all over campus. Don't you think everyone would enjoy an occasional peal of musical notes signaling the time of day or a special event?"

The responses were sometimes positive but often vaguely discouraging: "I wonder if the students would even appreciate it." "It's a good idea but probably too expensive." "There must be some problem with doing it. Otherwise, someone would have done it before."

Liesl refused to be dispirited. She decided to move forward as a one-woman committee. The campus engineer volunteered to check the structure and identify the electrical wiring requirements for installing chimes. She went online to research national companies that sell electrical chimes, and she selected two. Both companies expressed interest in making a bid to do the installation. She swallowed hard when both bids were in the $25,000 range. She would have to do some fundraising—an idea that held no appeal for her.

"I'm shy, maybe an introvert," she explains. "I had never tried raising money before. The idea stopped me cold. It turned me off. I put the work estimates in a drawer and tried to forget the idea.

"After a month, I realized nothing had changed. I was still the one-woman committee. I needed to step up. I contributed $1,000 from my savings to create the Tower Chimes Fund at the college. I made a list of those who might consider contributing, then began the uncomfortable one-on-one communications. Surprisingly, a professor, an administrator, and another volunteer quickly offered to match my gift. Suddenly, the fund was at $4,000. They also agreed to be my finance committee. Within six months, we had pledges for $27,000, and we ordered the chimes."

The following year, during Welcome Week, the chimes were scheduled for dedication and the inaugural ringing. The president gave a short speech, thanking the volunteers and donors, and then unveiled a new plaque on the tower, reading: "Liesl's Bell Tower."

The button was pushed. The chimes rang out over the campus and beyond.

"I cried," Liesl admits. The chimes will ring out across campus to unknown future generations. She fulfilled a want and left a legacy just by asking effectively and spotlighting her dream.

Tony and Liesl both asked for help. Tony, to help himself conquer drug addiction; Liesl to help others experience the inspirational joy of the chimes. Both achieved their goals by accepting a personal challenge, not giving up, and staying focused.

Circle of Wants

Starting with the heart and moving clockwise, the Circle of Wants symbols represent love, money, opportunity, health and justice.

THE CIRCLE OF WANTS

Circles are useful in illustrating wants and relationships. We often refer to circles of family, friends, business networks, church groups, help and support. HOW TO ASK adds the Circle of Wants and Circles of People to graphically illustrate important concepts in learning how to ask more effectively.

Your Circle of Wants is a visual expression of the money, love, opportunity, health, and justice you need and desire. Each of these wants is expressed with a familiar symbol in the illustration to the left. These symbols are repeated twice in the circle. Freely add all of your other wants to the circle with a word or symbol, whether they seem easily attainable just by asking effectively or seem out of reach. Always keep in mind that you are at its center.

CIRCLES OF PEOPLE

Circles of People illustrate networks of individuals who connect and relate through well-maintained lines of communication.

Social media offers instant, ever-expanding circles of friends, acquaintances, business contacts, and people with similar interests. Of course, there are good and bad circles. Some are a waste of time, or worse, turn good intentions into stolen identities and other negative outcomes. Internet circles will never replace eye contact, body language, and personal engagement. Yet, they can be a very helpful tool when used wisely.

This very day, you can expand the network of people who can help fulfill your wants. Select these people thoughtfully. Many people are not interested in or capable of giving you help, no matter how often you ask for it. Don't waste your time or theirs.

By expanding the number of people you can ask effectively for help, you are energizing your Circle of People. The rewards include more influence, more benefits flowing to you, and more charity flowing to others.

Start by visualizing yourself as a part of many separate network circles. Call these "people circles" that constantly enlarge, collapse, and reconfigure as people move in and out of them, either purposely or due to circumstance. To ask effectively, you must begin linking the people in your circles. The rewards may exceed your grandest expectations.

Linking Circles of People

The people-centered network circle is the most common tool that we use in life and communication. You already belong to many satellite circles evolving from family, jobs, sports, faith activities, hobbies, volunteering—wherever you participate in activities involving other people. When we look closely at these circles, three different models emerge:

• **Unlinked Model.** In this model, you network within each circle but do not link network circles. You do not introduce members of one circle to members of another. This is the least effective model.

• **Partially Linked Model.** In this model, you network within each circle and link some network circles together. Links may be to circles. You selectively or randomly introduce members of linked circles. The strength of the links and depth of the relationships will depend on the degree to which individuals proactively follow up on them. This is often the most effective model to fulfill your wants and the wants of others.

• **Fully Linked Model.** In this model, you network within each circle and link all network circles to one central circle. Links may be to multiple circles. You selectively or randomly introduce all members of linked circles to each other through the central circle. Without a carefully considered strategy, this model creates chaos. Yet if there is a need to quickly develop a giant network circle, as in politics or for a special event, this model can bring large groups together quickly. Graphics on the following pages visualize each model. Stories illustrate.

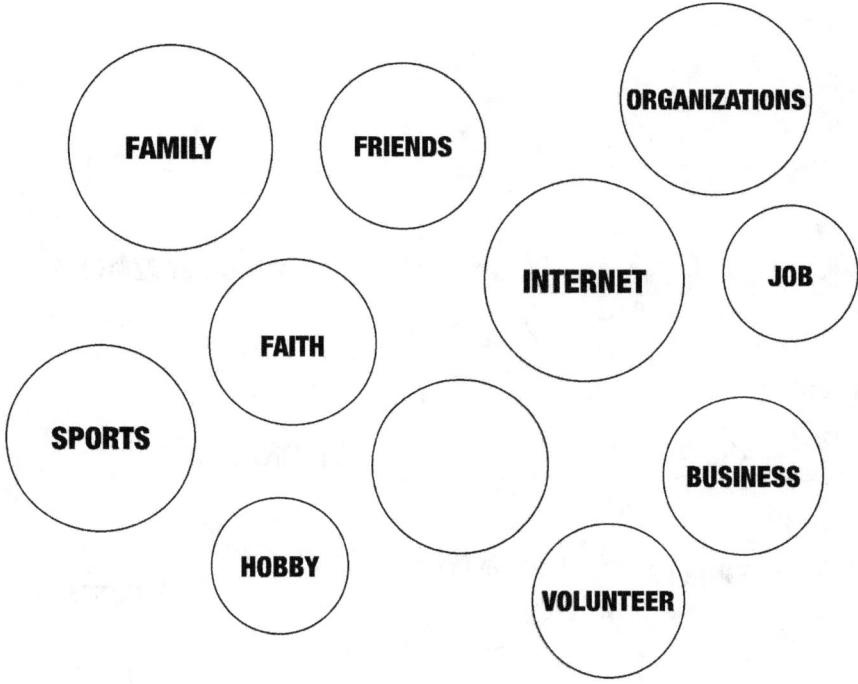

Unlinked Circles: In this model, you network within each circle, but do not link network circles. You do not introduce members of one circle to members of another. The blank circle encourages adding networks.

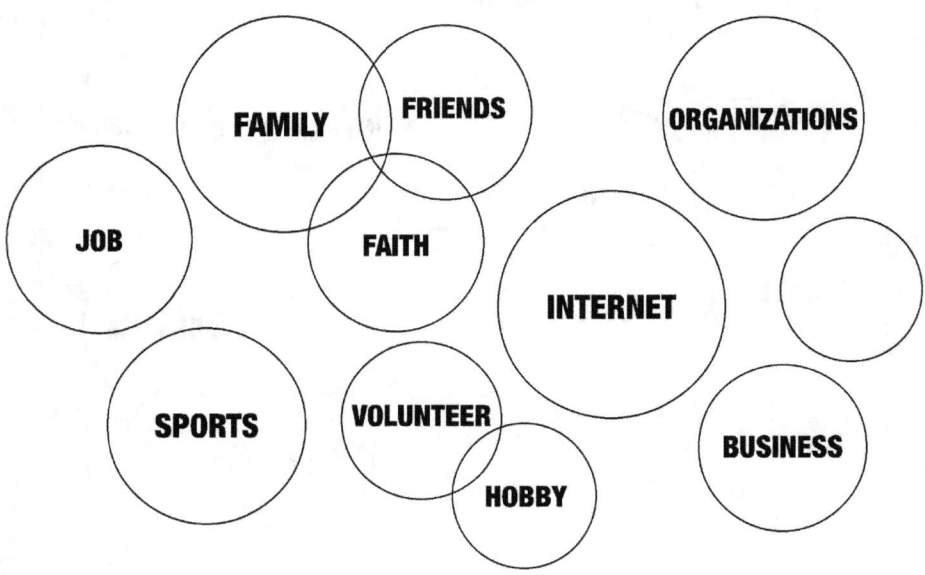

Partially Linked Circles: In this model, you network within each circle and link some network circles together. You selectively or randomly introduce members of linked circles to each other. Links may be to multiple circles. The blank circle encourages adding networks.

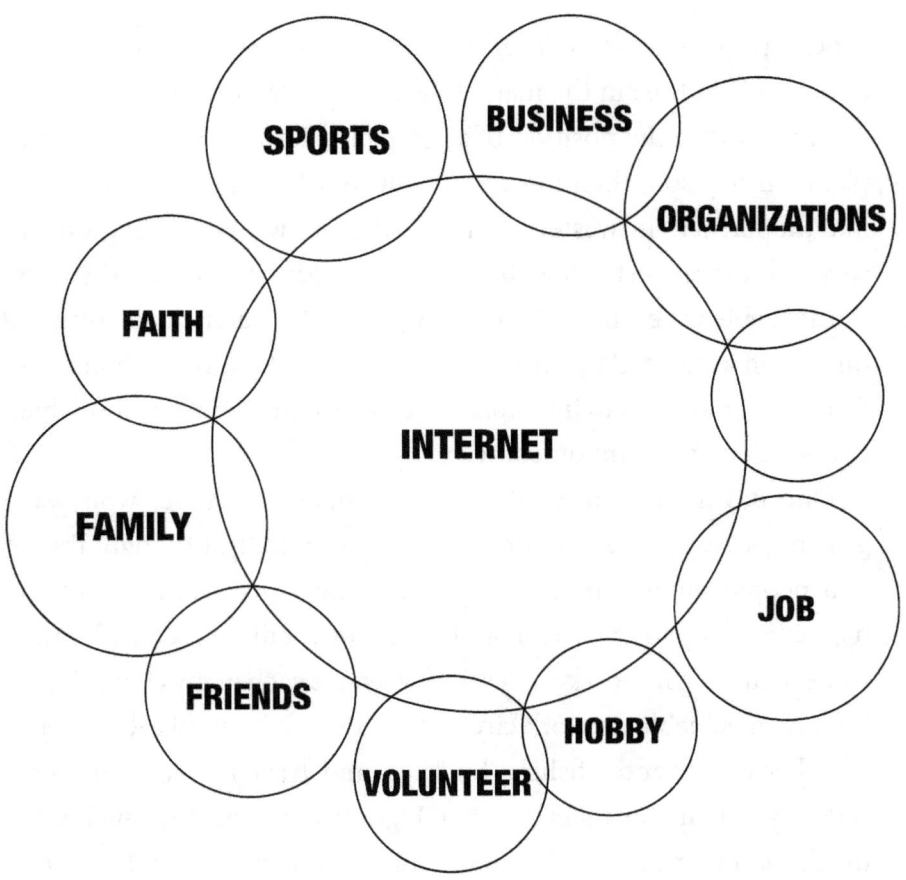

Fully Linked Circles: In this model, you network within each circle and link all network circles to one central circle. Links may be to multiple circles. You selectively or randomly introduce all members of linked circles to each other through the central circle. The blank circle encourages adding networks.

Big R's Circle of People

"I need a reliable source of money to take advantage of the investment opportunities I see in the marketplace," Big R lamented.

Big R was in the position of a struggling farmer who plows and plants in dry soil, then hopes for rain. But he wanted to be more like the farmers in western Kansas, who know that drilling down several hundred feet below their parched fields will connect them to the available water in the Ogallala Aquifer. The water can be turned on and off as needed by pushing the electric well button. Water is to farmers as money is to investors: A reliable source must be available to assure an abundant outcome.

One day I introduced Big R to a client, Mr. Mac, who was growing a very successful service business. Initially, I thought these two people might simply enjoy each other's acquaintance. (This happened early in my career, and at the time, I did not consider the value of linking network circles. I now realize each of my clients have their own valuable network circles.) As it turned out, Big R and Mr. Mac became friends, fishing buddies, and traveling companions. But they also did business together. Figuratively speaking, Big R was the dry land farmer, Mr. Mac the source of reliable water. Together, they grew and harvested bigger and better crops. They formed real estate investment partnerships, making strategic investments that neither would have visualized or completed separately. And as a result, they made many millions of dollars together and traveled to exotic places around the world.

Olivia's Circle of People

Olivia, a client, reflected on what it had been like as a single person again, after her husband's death.

I was miserable for nearly five years. I had no social life whatsoever. I spent my days working part-time as a teacher's aide, and my nights and weekends trying to guide my teenage son through puberty. My friends invited me to parties and other events, but I was often the only single person there and usually ended up sitting by myself in a corner, feeling lonely and isolated. I began to doubt that I would ever again have someone to share my heart with.

Then, while reading my church's bulletin one Sunday after services, I came across a little blurb about a singles group sponsored by the church. Each month the group held a potluck dinner and social in a room called The Gathering Place.

I thought about it for a moment, and then decided that for me, a singles group would probably be a waste of time. I didn't even know how to open myself up emotionally to men anymore. I put the bulletin—and the idea—away. But over the next few days, I found my thoughts wandering back to the group. I wanted to go, yet I didn't want to go.

Finally, I started asking myself some hard questions. Did I really want to spend the rest of my life without a partner to love? If not, what was I doing about it? How did I see my situation five years from now? Would I be happy with it? I realized I had to make some changes and stop feeling sorry for myself. I had to reach out and meet new people—people who might understand my struggles and share my yearnings.

It wasn't easy, but I made up my mind to attend a meeting of the singles group. I even baked an apple pie to bring along. During the hour-long social after dinner, I met some wonderful, supportive people. Several had been widowed. Others were divorced. Some had never had a partner to begin with. I had a great time—a feeling I hadn't enjoyed in years—and decided I would make the group a regular part of my life. After a few more meetings, I shared my heartbreak over losing my husband with other members, and some of them did the same with me—particularly one guy named Matthew, a recent divorcée who seemed kind of sweet—and I have to admit, very attractive.

Pretty soon I found myself thinking about him between meetings. He must have been having the same experience, because at the very next meeting, he asked me if I'd like to continue sharing our personal stories over breakfast the following morning at my favorite restaurant. "I'd love to," I said.

Six months later, we married. That was two years ago. And we're still so much in love I can hardly believe it. We're looking forward to a long and wonderful future together.

Olivia's way of effectively asking for help was to reach out to a new social circle, and the wonderful rewards she received in return were obvious in the joyful way she smiled as she finished her story.

Dr. Milt in My Circle

"You must take your baby to the hospital emergency room tonight. He has a severe case of RSV," Dr. Milt instructed my daughter. He had stopped by my home to pick up a ski boot left in my car after a recent day together, and coincidentally, my daughter's family was visiting. I had taken the opportunity to ask Dr. Milt to do a quick examination of Ethan, our new grandchild, because the baby had a fever that continued upward, plus other flu-like symptoms.

For most infants, respiratory syncytial virus (RSV) causes an illness that resembles a common cold, but some babies are at high risk for a more severe form of the disease. Serious RSV can lead to dangerous complications, including lung infections. Symptoms include coughing and wheezing, gasping for breath, caved-in chest, bluish skin color, and a high fever.

Ethan had some of these symptoms and a temperature of 102° F. With RSV, pneumonia, other complications and even death could occur quickly.

My daughter and her husband bundled their baby in a warm blanket and rushed to the hospital. It was 9 p.m., on a dark, cold December night. Dr. Milt called ahead and talked to someone in the emergency room. He told them there was a 1-month-old baby on the way who could not wait to be treated. The child would need intensive pediatric care immediately.

An emergency room nurse was waiting at the door. Ethan was quickly taken to the infant care area on the third floor. A hospitalist listened to his tiny heart and lungs, then put him on oxygen and intravenous feeding. They kept a ventilator on standby. There was no other treatment. Antibiotics are useless against RSV.

Mother and father paced the night away at the hospital, waiting and watching. Slowly, Ethan's fever came down, his color improved, and his coughing subsided. Assuring phone calls were made to family members. Anxiety changed to relief. Ethan eventually made a full recovery.

Dr. Milt is a part of my skiing circle. Every February, a group of us rent a house at Vail, Aspen, Big Sky, or another ski resort for a "boys' ski together." Dr. Milt and I had become close friends while driving together to ski destinations, riding chair lifts, and sharing kitchen duties. Now, we meet regularly for breakfast, share life experiences, and help each other. He provides medical advice, and I provide legal guidance. Most importantly, we are friends.

Valuable Network Circle Members

A good healthcare provider is a valuable person to include in one of your network circles. Medical doctors, nurses, pharmacists, dentists, healthcare administrators, personal trainers, massage therapists, or anyone else with specialized healthcare knowledge can improve—even save—your life, or that of a loved one or friend. Having them in your circle is a win-win for all concerned.

Healthcare providers also need networks. Often, their daily routines are intense and isolating. Invite them to join one of your network circles.

Valuable network circles make asking effective in every life endeavor. Think of personal interests and needs as diverse as financial planning, fundraising, religious faith, bridge tournaments and neighborhood watches. Use network circles to fulfill needs and desires.

Part III

Priceless Insights

GET INSIGHTS

"Discovery consists of seeing what everybody has seen and thinking what nobody has thought."
—Albert Szent-Gyorgyi, scientist

Robert Blendon, professor of health policy and political analysis at the Harvard University School of Public Health, has said, "We live in a complex world, and understanding things is an enormous challenge." Enormous challenges may lead to enormous rewards. Understanding the factors that contribute to fulfilling wants successfully is one of those enormous challenges.

This following section, like the entire book, relies on insights. In the opinion of many with more knowledge and wisdom than I, insight is the most important outcome of all thought. The Old Testament of the Bible reinforces this observation: "The beginning of wisdom is this: Get wisdom, and whatever else you get, get insight." (Proverbs 4:7.)

COMMONPLACING

The great minds of the 17th and 18th centuries, such as John Milton, Francis Bacon, and John Locke, developed the practice of maintaining a personal "commonplace" book. Scholars, amateur scientists, aspiring writers, and actors—virtually all groups marked by intellectual ambition—were likely to keep a commonplace book. These books were used as personal journals. The custom had the advantage of encouraging the reader to become engaged in reflecting on the meaning of a topic.

In 1652, John Locke began maintaining a commonplace book during his first year at Oxford. Simultaneously, he developed an elaborate system for indexing the book's content. He emphasized this system in his classic work, "An Essay Concerning Human Understanding." "When I meet with anything that I think fit to put into my commonplace book," Locke observed, "I first find a proper head."

In its most customary form, "commonplacing," as it was called, involved transcribing interesting or inspirational passages from observations and reading. The result became a personal encyclopedia of observations and quotations. Steven Johnson, author of Where Good Ideas Come From, observed, "There is a distinct self-help quality to the early descriptions of commonplacing's virtues: maintaining the books enabled one to 'lay up a fund of knowledge, from which we may at all times select what is useful in the several pursuits of life.'" The Bible is the most referenced commonplace book ever published. The books and chapters are credited to various prophets, apostles, and disciples, so that the entirety is a collection of observations and stories written over a 1600-year period. The information collectors came from many walks of life. Among them were farmers, fishermen, shepherds, doctors, prophets, judges, and kings.

When the Bible was assembled, the goal was to collect the most important and insightful writings, stories, and histories into a single book that would provide enough content for any person to study and understand God's message. Its anecdotal style, using short, observational narratives of biographical incidents, has proven timelessly compelling.

The Old Testament came from stories handed down by word of mouth in the Middle East. Later, these stories were written down by scholars and scribes. Generally speaking, Christians acknowledge that the exact wording in the New Testament was executed by human authors and transcribers, but that all the writing was inspired by God.

The Bible, like every commonplace collection, is not a linear book to be read page after page, cover to cover. Rather, it is a resource from which we may select what is important and helpful in the pursuit of life on Earth and in the hereafter.

Charles Darwin's notebooks evidenced the "commonplace" tradition. Phillip Johnson, author of Darwin on Trial, concluded that Darwin's ideas evolved because he had adhered to a rigorous practice of maintaining notebooks in which he quoted other sources, improvised new ideas, examined and dismissed false leads, drew diagrams, and generally let his mind roam. He constantly revisited his notes, discovering new implications.

Darwin's breakthrough in the theories of natural selection and evolution occurred several years after recording much of his accumulated learning in these notebooks. He first had to travel the intellectual journey to the edge of existing knowledge before he could take the next step into the unknown. His notebooks became a platform on which he could rearrange the pieces of an ever-expanding puzzle, hoping the separate pieces would eventually begin to fit together. And they did.

As it did for Darwin, the commonplace book even today can serve as a record of thoughts that come up in a search for new ways to link information. For example, by linking new scientific discoveries, advances in technology, and human responses to both, apparent chaos may be reassembled in systematic order that offers meaning.

When you turn on your electronic device, you are using it as an electronic commonplace book to store personal observations and quotes by, about, from, and to yourself and others. The Internet, with all its search engines and applications, connects the past with the present and opens new pathways to the future. It allows information that initially appeared chaotic to engender logical systems that lead to new understandings. Google, Facebook, Twitter, LinkedIn, and thousands of Internet outlets serve as contemporary commonplace books. New ones appear daily (and sometimes make their creators into billionaires). The stories, anecdotes, quotes, and observations in this book have been selected not because each has "ask" stamped on it, but because each offers useful observations about some facet of successfully asking for, or offering, help to fulfill wants. Remember, this is not a linear book to be read methodically from beginning to end. Instead, it is a resource from which you may select what is important and helpful to you. It may also act as a model you can use in creating your own commonplace book.

WIT AND WISDOM

Humor comes close to being a Win Word in my Commonplace Book. It may make the final cut in yours. It's at least a corollary, an important addition to all the basics, and a valuable tool in every good negotiator's toolbox.

Big R always finishes difficult negotiations with a broad smile and often a hardy laugh. His quick change in facial expression disarms everyone at the table. A humorous comment or story distracts people from focusing on differences. Stress melts into a shared feeling of relief. Humor allows unaccommodating discussions to continue. A common ground of accommodation is often only one or two laughs away.

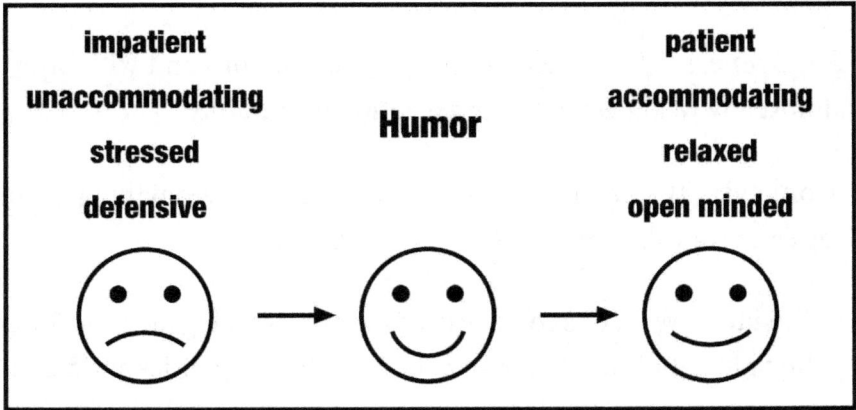

In my own life, with family and friends, as a counselor-at-law, and in leadership positions on local, state, and national boards, I have tried always to use humor as a catalyst. When participating in a contentious meeting, for example, I often prepare by writing a few humorous one-liners on a piece of paper that I slip into my pocket. Remembering jokes is not my strong suit. Occasionally, I will glance at my humor crib sheet during the meeting.

Will Rogers

To keep it simple and add historical interest with perspective, I often quote Will Rogers, an uneducated cowboy, humorist, movie star, author, and political commentator. I may most commonly share his observations that "Everybody is ignorant, only on different subjects," and "A man only learns by two things. One is reading, and the other is association with smart people."

Consider other remarks by this self-described "illiterate cowboy."

Payment and costs: "It's not what you pay a man, but what he costs you that counts."

Common sense: "You can't legislate intelligence and common sense into people."

Forgiveness: "The American people are generous and will forgive almost any weakness with the exception of stupidity."

Monkeys: "There's still a lot of monkey in us. Throw anything in our cage and we will give it serious consideration."

Politicians: "What this country needs is more working men and fewer politicians. Abolish salaries and you will abolish politics and taxes."

Honesty: "Let's be honest with ourselves and not take ourselves too seriously, and never condemn the other fellow for doing what we are doing every day, only in a different way."

Change: "People's minds are changed through observation and not through argument."

Prosperity: "We can't go through life just eating cake all the time. We like prosperity but we are having so much of it that we just can't afford it."

Next door: "That's one trouble with our charities. We are always saving someone away off, when the fellow next door ain't eating."

Taxes: "This is income tax paying day. When it's made out, you don't know if you are a crook or a martyr."

Progress: "We do more talking progress than we do progressing."

Humility: "My own mother died when I was 10 years old. My folks have told me that what little humor I have comes from her. I can't remember her humor. I can remember her love and understanding of me."

Likability: "I joked about every prominent man of my time, but I never met a man I didn't like."

Arnold R. Weber

Arnold R. Weber's résumé lists many accomplishments. Three U.S. presidents sought his sage counsel and appointed him to high economic and labor problem-solving positions. As president of the University of

Colorado and Northwestern University, he led both institutions to new levels of excellence. Financial confidante to super-wealthy and famous families, he mediated complex intergenerational conflicts and helped manage billions of dollars of assets. His greatest talent in doing so was to combine wit with wisdom.

Arnie and I became friends while I was chairman of the University of Colorado Board of Regents. During these years, we worked closely on several headline news issues. In our subsequent 25 years of friendship, I have watched and listened as he has effectively led charges to excellence whenever and wherever the bugle sounded. His winning strategies always have included humor to make angry people laugh and ugly choices acceptable. Arnie once confided with a smile, "My goal in life is to find the ultimate one-liner."

A few of his remarks illustrate.

After making a difficult decision: "There is a big difference between feeling good and being effective."

To graduating students: "If you're going to be the tail of the kite, make sure it's attached to a high flyer."

When raising money: "Always open your mail. You never know when something good will be in it. Always return phone calls. A nascent benefactor may be waiting."

In negotiations: "Never negotiate with yourself. Never make a deal you can't afford to walk away from."

When managing a budget: "The time to manage tough is when things are good. You don't become beloved by running a tight budget."

Quoting former U.S. Sen. Everett Dirksen on making decisions

based on a moral foundation: "I am a man of principle, and my first principle is flexibility."

After lobbying state legislators for funding higher education: "I spend so much time touching base, I'm not even in the game. It involves politics and money, and that's two ways of saying the same thing."

In answer to a question on the unfunded costs of future higher education: "Well, we'll cross that bridge when it collapses."

A humble presidential analogy: "Being the president of a major university is sort of like being a coal miner in 19th-century England. You spend a lot of time on your hands and knees, groping in the dark, dodging lumps of coal, and bumping into walls. Every now and then you get some coal to the surface and you really feel satisfaction … Although that may seem rich in potential, it's not a very efficient way of doing things."

Ronald Reagan

Our nation's 40th president, Ronald Reagan, placed great importance on wit with wisdom. Historian Douglas Brinkley observed, "If Reagan went out to dinner with somebody in New York or Sacramento, and in the course of a long dinner, someone told a really funny joke, or something struck him as humorous, he would write it down on a note card. When he needed an anecdote to add sparkle to a speech, he relied on his cards."

Often referred to as The Great Communicator or the Teflon President, Reagan was famous for his self-deprecating wit. He loved jokes, quips, and one-liners. Some of his memorable quotations include:

"It's hard when you are up to your armpits in alligators to remember you came [to Washington] to drain the swamp."

"It's true that hard work never killed anyone, but I figure, why take the chance?"

"I have wondered what the Ten Commandments would have looked like if Moses would have run them through Congress."

"There are advantages to being elected president. The day after I was elected, I had my high school grades classified as top secret."

"Politics is just like show business. You have a hell of an opening, coast for a while, then have a hell of a close."

"We were poor when I was young. But the difference then was the government didn't come around telling you you were poor."

And to his wife, Nancy, after he was shot in an assassination attempt: "Honey, I forgot to duck."

Barack Obama

Barack Obama, our 44th president, tended to add deadpan flourishes to his punchlines. He would make small changes that made a difference, such as a look or a pause. He used humor to humanize himself.

"If I had to name my greatest strength, I guess it would be my humility. Greatest weakness: It's possible I'm a little too awesome."

On attacks on him at the 2008 Republican convention: "I've been called worse on the basketball court."

"What a week. As some of you heard, the state of Hawaii released my long-form birth certificate. Hope this puts all doubts to rest. But just in case there are any lingering questions, tonight I'm going to go a step farther. Tonight, for the first time, I am releasing my official birth video."

"I know Republicans are still sorting out what happened in 2012. But one thing they all agree on is they need to do a better job reaching out to minorities. And look, call me self-centered, but I can think of one minority they could start with."

"Honestly, there wasn't a lot of room for advancement in my last job [as president]. The only one with a more powerful position was my wife."

Other Powerful Observations about Wit With Wisdom:

"If you lose the power to laugh, you lose the power to think."
—Clarence Darrow, lawyer

"Life is like a blanket too short. You pull it up and your toes rebel, you yank it down and shivers meander about your shoulders; but cheerful folks manage to draw their knees up and pass a very comfortable night."
—Marion Howard, artist

"I know God will not give me anything I can't handle. I just wish that He didn't trust me so much."
—Mother Teresa, humanitarian

"If you don't get everything you want, think of the things you don't get that you don't want."
—Oscar Wilde, author

"As long as the world is turning and spinning, we're gonna be dizzy, and we're gonna make mistakes."
—Mel Brooks, film director, comedian

"It's kind of fun to do the impossible."
—Walt Disney, founder of the Walt Disney Company

"If people concentrated on the really important things in life, there'd be a shortage of fishing poles."
—Doug Larson, author

"Every time is a time for comedy in a world of tension that would languish without it. But I cannot confine myself to lightness in a period of human life that demands light. We all know that, as the old adage has it, 'It is later than you think'…but I also say occasionally, "It is lighter than you think.' In this light let's not look back in anger, or forward in fear, but around in awareness."
—James Thurber, humorist and cartoonist

"Not a shred of evidence exists in favor of the idea that life is serious."
—Brendan Gill, writer

"Money is not the most important thing in the world. Love is. Fortunately, I love money."
—Jackie Mason, comedian

"He who does not like wine, song, and wife, remains a fool for the whole of his life."
—Martin Luther, theologian

"Life would be tragic if it weren't funny."
—Stephen Hawking, physicist

"No problem is too big to run away from."
—Charles M. Schulz, cartoonist

"The sun don't shine on the same dog's ass all the time."
—Jim "Catfish" Hunter, Major League Baseball pitcher

A personal favorite anecdote about "the perfect husband":
Several men are in the locker room of a golf club. A cell phone on a bench rings, and a man engages the hands-free speaker function and begins to talk. Everyone else in the room stops to listen.
Man: "Hello?"
Woman: "Hi Honey, it's me. Are you at the club?"
Man: "Yes."
Woman: "I was shopping and found this beautiful leather coat. It's only $2,000. Is it OK if I buy it?"
Man: "Sure, go ahead if you like it that much."
Woman: "I also stopped by the Cadillac dealership and looked at all the new models. I saw one I really liked."
Man: "How much?"
Woman: "$75,000."
Man: "OK, but for that price I want it with all the options."
Woman: "Great! Oh, and one more thing. I was just talking to Janie and found out that the house I wanted last year is back on the market. They're asking $980,000 for it."
Man: "Well, then go ahead and make an offer of $900,000. They'll probably take it. If not, we can go the extra $80,000 if it's what you really want."
Woman: "OK. I'll see you later! I love you so much!"
Man: "Bye! I love you, too."
The man hangs up. The other men in the locker room are staring at him in astonishment, mouths wide open.
He turns and asks, "Anyone know whose phone this is?"

BOTTOM UPPERS and TOP DOWNERS

To fulfill our wants, we must effectively ask responsive people for help. By responsive people, I mean the open-minded, open-hearted individuals who cross your path daily. They may be candidly looking for help themselves, or quietly waiting and watching for a meaningful circumstance to help others. These are the bottom uppers.

They are responsive because, consciously or subconsciously, they also have unfulfilled wants. They may be climbing the business ladder, pulling themselves up one rung at a time, or in need of an affordable, accessible healthcare provider, or a friend they can call late at night to laugh or cry with. They may have free time to volunteer. They are searching for opportunities to validate their potential.

Bottom uppers may offer a service (anything from housecleaning to legal advice), a relationship (from being a social contact to a romantic partner), information (from gardening tips to investment advice), networks (from job opportunities to Internet links). These moments of connection do not announce themselves by drum or trumpet. They occur during common everyday events.

In contrast to the bottom uppers are the top downers. These individuals perceive themselves as successful, privileged, and entitled.

They circulate within networks of other top downers. Seldom do they socialize with the bottom uppers. They prefer control, relegating the bottom uppers to a subservient status in their activities. Their wants are influenced by their peers. Their friends must be like-minded. They resist social mobility.

It is difficult, often impossible, to satisfy the needs and expectations of these folks. Their unfulfilled wants create fractured families. Their accountants, bankers, lawyers, even their medical doctors and golf partners, feel the stress. Often, their advisors are one step away from being replaced. Top downers are not open-minded, open-hearted folks who make a difference in your life.

A story involving a client comes to mind.

Scott Was Never Satisfied

Scott started as a bottom upper. He worked as a financial planner selling insurance and annuities and managing investment portfolios. Although he was moderately successful, after a few years, he became frustrated by comparing his lifestyle to that of his high-net-worth friends. He was good-looking, well liked, and athletic, but none of those advantages satisfied him. He decided he needed to access the top downers to accelerate his career.

He moved his family into a McMansion, a three-story colonial house on a landscaped half-acre, surrounded by similar homes. He began to solicit old-wealth clients. He asked to be accepted, but he found the social and financial firewalls difficult to penetrate. He borrowed money to keep up appearances. Debt led to stress. Eventually, his marriage imploded. His second marriage, to a like-minded woman, blew up when they both realized they were not fulfilling each other's top down wants. Today, he is deeply in debt, unmarried, lonely, and miserable. His children, from his first marriage, are confused and angry with him. And he is still not a top downer. Why he or anyone else would want to be one, is beyond me.

Jack Was Surprised

A while back, I was helping Jack, another rags-to-riches client, with his real estate portfolio. He described fascinating snippets of his life as we made small talk examining real estate documents.

> Been married 50 years and have six children and 12 grandchildren. Married the best-looking girl in my high school class.
> I was working as a lineman for the telephone company and wanted to do better for my family. One day, I was working below ground, in a manhole, repairing wires. A coworker told me about a job selling office equipment. Next day, I applied for the job. Surprisingly, I got it. I learned the business, then started my own office equipment company. Sold that business 20 years later and started buying apartment buildings.
> I love what I do. No plans to retire, but I need your help to set up an intergenerational family partnership. I want to help my grandchildren through college, careers, whatever."

Jack continues to be a bottom upper, still reaching out for help and providing help to others.

More Stories

Bottom uppers and top downers are not necessarily differentiated by wealth or status. Dan, at age 45, owns and operates a one-person, one-room, storefront watch repair shop. He bought the shop 15 years ago with money borrowed from his parents. During his years of ownership, he has never painted a wall, or replaced a worn, dirty rug. Inventory has slowly declined. He now keeps part of his beer can collection in the display counter next to a few secondhand watches. He smokes and sells cigarettes. His main business has changed from selling and repairing watches to primarily replacing batteries. Store hours are sporadic. His two-year marriage has floundered, then dissolved. He declines invitations to join in extended family gatherings. He spends weekends picking through abandoned trash dumps in search of old beer cans to add to his collection. Dan is a top downer because he never asks for help and never offers any.

Recently, I attended an annual luncheon for over 100 people actively engaged in the business side of my local community. This was the 20th such meeting. Each person was asked to stand and give a brief activities update. Ken, confined to a wheelchair by a stroke, spoke two words into the microphone. "Recovering lawyer."

What did he mean by this? Before his stroke, Ken had been a bottom-up lawyer serving top-down clients. He worked with high-net-worth people—often those with inherited wealth—and a bank that served these people. He candidly reflected that he could never satisfy these people. They were always in a hurry and complained about his fees.

I asked him if he missed the practice of law. "Not for a minute," he grimaced. It's not surprising that he had been unhappy in his career and now felt as if he had to "recover" from it.

People, intentionally or otherwise, sometimes change from bottom uppers to top downers, or from top downers to bottom uppers. A few transition back and forth because of life events and social or workplace variables that seem to blow them about like a typhoon at sea. These folks often become confused and conflicted as they struggle with changing wants. Marriages often fall victim to their individual struggles.

But again, despite the apparent complexity of these changes, the difference between the two personality types is simple: Bottom uppers ask personally for help and offer help to others. Top downers do not ask personally for help or offer help to others. Being a top downer or bottom upper is not determined by wealth, privilege, power, or social status. It is a choice made by each individual.

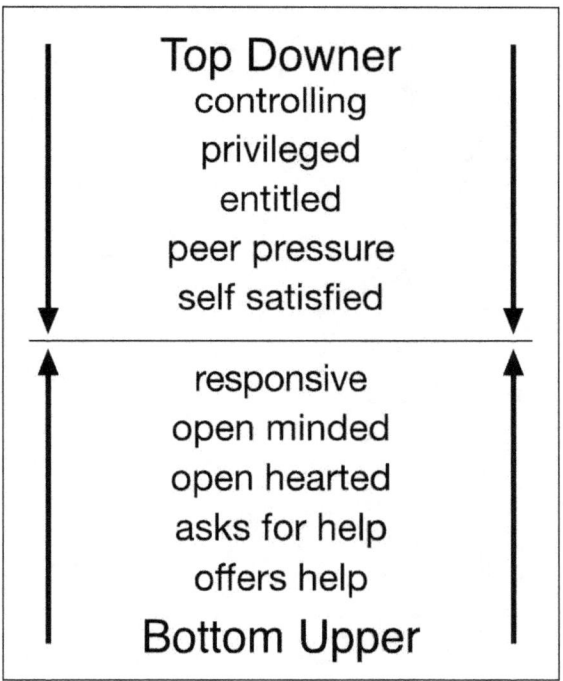

BE VULNERABLE

One morning, during a breakfast meeting with Big R, the conversation eventually turned to effective asking. There was a point I had been thinking about for a while.

"With all of the advantages there are to asking for what you want, there must be risks, too—don't you think?" I asked.

"I do," he replied. "I think it makes you vulnerable."

"Why? Because you risk rejection?" I probed.

"Exactly," he affirmed. "You're telling someone you need help to resolve a problem, to successfully conclude a negotiation."

"Interesting point. I wonder how you could reduce that risk?"

"Well, the obvious way would be not to make yourself vulnerable to begin with. Asking requires a certain amount of self-confidence. Self-esteem. People with no self-confidence are generally ineffective askers. If you ask for what you want, I don't think you can avoid risk—but you can manage it."

"How so?"

"Strategic timing. Wait for the right moment to ask for help. Be willing to back off, be patient, redirect the conversation. Remember, you are inviting others to believe in you. Believing is a feeling. The desire to help flows from using the essential 5 Win Words during personal, one-on-one experiences. Effective asking should engender feelings of believing. But it takes time for two people to get to that point in their relationship."

"So it's that simple?"

"Yep. That simple. Also, people who ask can't take themselves too seriously. Learning to fail successfully takes practice. If you are rejected, wait for the next strategic time. Try again, or move on. Find the need and you will succeed."

As always, ideas are best illustrated with examples. Consider the power of vulnerability. Jesus Christ, Abraham Lincoln, John F. Kennedy, and Martin Luther King Jr., all paid the ultimate price for vulnerability. They exemplify asking at the highest level. They asked effectively for people to follow them, while simultaneously offering help to others. They asked others to believe in them. They accepted the risks that flow from vulnerability.

But these are the extreme cases. In our everyday lives, we can be vulnerable without being martyrs. Simple expressions such as "I love you," "Hello, my friend," and "Drive safely," show you care. As with asking, to care is to show vulnerability. The risk you take, of course, is being met with indifference, ambivalence, or rejection. If that happens, wait for another strategic moment, ask for help, and offer help again. Eventually you will feel the warmth. You will hear inviting words. You will begin fulfilling your wants.

Tony Stopped Trying

Tony was in my office to discuss the estate of his stepmother, Ava. She had left more of it to him than to her nieces and nephews because, as he put it, "Ava knew I liked money." His story could be titled "No Risk, No Reward."

"She must have had great affection for you," I said.

"I'm not sure what I'll do with the inheritance. I'm single. I'm 47 years old, and I've never been married. It's a lonely life. At least Ava and Dad had each other."

Tony was a nice-looking guy, a community college graduate who operated a small business from his home. He was also working toward a private pilot's license.

"Add some romance," I suggested.

"Tried that," he said. "I was engaged to someone I'd known for a long time, but then she backed out—called it off for no reason. After that, she moved to Florida. I flew there several times to visit her, but she married another guy within six months. I'm not looking anymore."

"There are always more fish in the sea," I said. "Have you tried an online dating service? They do the looking for you."

"Nope. Not interested."

Our next meeting was all business. Even with his new inheritance, he was not going to open the vulnerability door again, not going to risk another rejection.

Do you know any Tonys? Are you a Tony when it comes to asking for a pay increase or a friendly favor? When offering an apology or searching for a new love? As vulnerability decreases, so do opportunities. Fewer risks, fewer rewards.

Personally, I feel the warmth. I know. Vulnerability pays off in lifetime dividends. Years ago, when I was young and single, two friends and I were cruising around the Denver social scene one evening. We stopped at a young people's hangout. I met a girl named Dorothy, a new teacher celebrating her first paycheck. I wrote her name and telephone number on a napkin and called her a few days later. We were both vulnerable. Today she is the charming, beautiful, smart mother of our three children, and grandmother to their children. Allowing myself to be vulnerable has certainly paid off in my life!

Do you take risks to fulfill wants?

THE LAW OF ONE

To ask effectively, you must apply the Law of One. The law is simple. Like all simple ideas, it crystallized personally after a great deal of contemplation and a long gestation period. Here is the law: Only One Person Matters! Identify the most important person in any given situation and deal one-on-one with him or her. Effective laws, like mathematical formulas, require validation. Consider the following proofs.

Love. We all search for love. We hope to love one person romantically, and in turn, we hope one person loves us, individually, forever. Most of our life comprises searching and then caring for "the one and only." We love each member of our family separately, differently. Marriage is a ceremony that confirms commitment, based on the Law of One.

Family. I grew up in a single-parent household. My divorced mother raised my two older sisters and me. I saw my father once in 41 years. By default, as the only adult, my mother was the one who made the decisions in our home. She struggled financially, and her life was further complicated by rheumatoid arthritis and a jack-hammer stutter. Her emotional engagements with life are a reminder to not expect perfection from the one making the decisions.

Friendships. My wife, Dorothy, and I enjoyed the friendship of Doug and Phyllis Warren for many years. Recently, the relationship became fractured over some differences on political issues. I suggested we have a big party and invite the Warrens. Dorothy countered, "We should invite only Doug and Phyllis for an informal, one-on-one supper and conversation." We did, and she was right. Our differences faded with individualized memories, family updates, laughter, and talk of future plans.

Jobs. If you are looking for a job, you may have answered hundreds of help-wanted ads without landing a position because you did not affirmatively connect with the one person who makes the final decisions. Instead of using a painter's spray gun, use an artist's fine brush when searching for opportunity. Write down what you enjoy doing, your qualifications, and a prioritized short list of preferred jobs. Identify the one person who controls the hire. Creatively access that person using every available resource. Communicate using the 5 Win Words. You will pass the competition on your way up.

Deals. Many of my clients make business deals. A deal can be anything where money and property change hands. Often, it takes years to judge the outcomes, to identify the winners and losers, the profit-and-loss leaders. From observing hundreds of transactions, the Law of One clearly applies. One person's vision conceptualizes the deal.

People in need. Vincent La France is my friend. He is a street person who has been asking to fulfill his wants on the same corner during lunchtime for 15 years, through summer heat and winter cold. He adds value by singing and playing a guitar. As I walk by, he always calls out with a smile, "Hi, Sandy." I respond with a wave and thumbs-up, and a "Good music, Vince!" Sometimes I drop a

$20 bill into his open guitar case. He lives by the Law of One—one giver at a time.

Justice. Early in my legal career, I represented numerous criminal defendants charged with felonies and misdemeanors. Some work was pro bono, which in lawyer lingo means "without pay." Twelve-, six-, and three-person juries decided the fate of my clients. I never lost a criminal jury trial. It was not because of brilliance or experience—I lacked both. I simply applied the Law of One. I only needed one juror to side with my client for a not guilty verdict.

Visualize the Law of One as a series of concentric circles. In the graphic on the following page, "A" represents the first circle of people you will encounter. Each more controlling circle is identified by "B," "C" and "D." The One who matters is in the center circle. No matter the number of circles, you must access The One in the center. This person is the decision-maker capable of satisfying a want. Direct access is preferable, but access through an intermediary can sometimes assist in producing a favorable outcome.

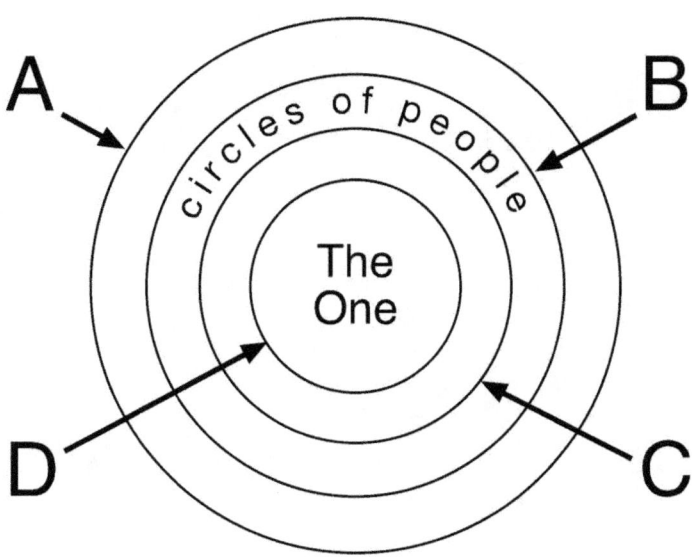

In our daily activities, often we falsely believe we cannot connect to The One. When we are in an outer circle, we must learn to communicate with people in the inner circles. When we are The One, we must know how to communicate with people in the outer circles.

To fulfill our wants, we must ask for help from others. Don't waste time wandering in the social, business, or workplace wilderness. Choose a person who has access to the inner circles, develop a relationship, and ask that person effectively for help. Continue until you access The One—the decision-maker. It will make all the difference.

TELL A STORY

Gran Canaria is one of the seven islands known as the Canary Islands located in the Atlantic Ocean, 93 miles off the northwest coast of Africa, and 838 miles from its mother country, Spain. It is a volcanic island with deep valleys, volcanic cones, and no yellow canaries.

Big R and I, with our wives, were vacation cruising toward the islands on the most famous ocean liner in the world, the *Queen Mary 2*. Big R was staying in a state room suite on the top guest floor. During one of our regular afternoon discussions, we asked ourselves what the very essence of effective asking might be.

"I think you have to tell stories," Big R said. "How well you tell your story determines what you get. You have to create trust. The listener must believe their best interest is most important to you. And to get to the right conclusion, you must tell the right story. You can be obnoxious, unattractive, a jerk, but if you tell the right story, with honesty and sincerity, you'll create a connection with the one important person you're talking to."

"But isn't storytelling a talent you're born with? How can someone become good at it if they don't do it naturally?" I asked him.

"Knowledge!" Big R said. "You have to know your subject matter. And you need some knowledge about your listener to predict how he or she will react to your story. The story must create an expectation. An expectation that a want of the listener will be satisfied. When I'm buying and selling real estate, I have a three-step formula I include in every story. I call it 'Tell and do.' The steps are: Tell a story the listener can relate to; lead to conclusions that are believable and doable; and come to closure."

"Okay, but that's kind of vague," I said. "Can you give me a real-life example?"

"Sure. Selling a starter house to a married couple, I tell them the story of another couple, very similar to themselves, who successfully bought a similar house. They qualified for a 20-year loan, got low interest, paid below market price for the property, and closed within 30 days. The property value has jumped 10 percent since closing. Everyone is happy. Good thing they did not procrastinate.

"Prospective homebuyers will immediately relate to this story and want to duplicate it. I tell it because I know enough about the buyers to believe I can make it happen. Then I do make it happen."

The following graph illustrates the importance of storytelling and trust.

I reflected on a recent case as counselor-at-law. Danny and his wife drove a twice-widowed new client, his stepmother, to my office to prepare a new will. Danny told me in advance that he was the caregiver and that he was going to receive all the inheritance. In a private, confidential conversation, my client advised that he had two children by his first marriage. He had not seen them in 10 years and seldom communicated with them, but he still cared about them. His request was that his will give equal shares to his two natural children and to Danny. He then stepped into the waiting room to have a word with Danny.

When the client came back a week later to sign his will, Danny waited with a scowl on his face. Danny's wife also glowered in the waiting room. Obviously, the gentleman had told Danny about the terms of his will.

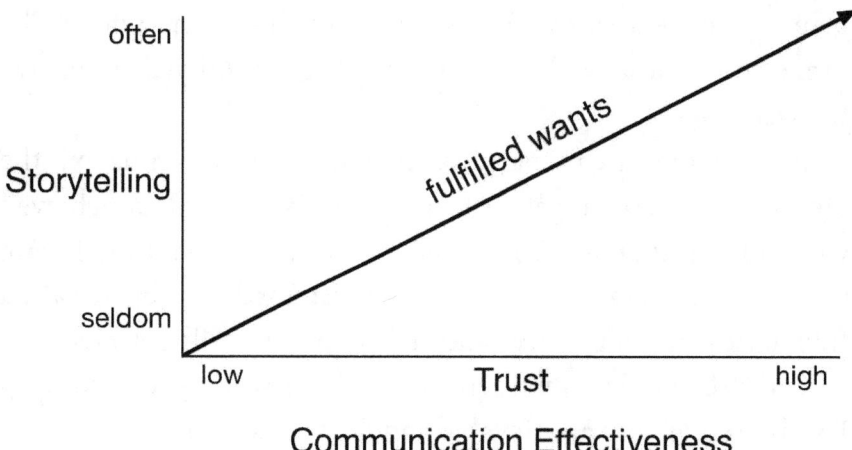

Communication Effectiveness

Six months later, the gentleman died. I met with Danny and told him it would be necessary to probate the will. He responded with a smile, "Oh no, I've taken care of it. I have been helping my stepfather manage his money and pay the bills. My name is on all his accounts. I'll take care of his other two children."

I am certain the two natural children received no inheritance. The will was worthless. Danny received all the accounts as the surviving joint owner. As I stated before, I call this "inheritance hijacking." This hijacking is nothing more than a heist without a gun. It is an increasing national, intergenerational scourge. Family feuds end in expensive probate court litigation—often too little, too late because the assets have disappeared. The perpetrators of stealth inheritance hijacking may be close caregivers or members of blended families (which seldom actually blend). The victims often never discover the hijacking has taken place.

I tell this story to my wills and trusts clients. They react with fear that they will not complete their own estate plans correctly and in time, and will fail to take care of their loved ones. The story guarantees a new paying client. On one Friday, one client told me he was worried about having not completed his estate plan before the weekend. He asked what to do. I responded, "The same thing you have been doing for the last 60 years: Survive the weekend."

When people are preparing wills and trusts, they must put the pieces of the puzzle together to assure their goals will be achieved when the need arises. To implement an intergenerational plan, the maker's intent is carried out. Trustworthy helpers, called fiduciaries, are imperative and should be carefully selected.

The "tell and do" approach will work for you if you follow Big R's three steps. Tell a believable and doable story. Tie the story to the listener's wants. Come to closure to convert wants into realities.

MANAGING ASKERS

"Can you manage askers? Who are the most powerful managers?" I once asked Big R.

"Mothers!" he replied without hesitation. "Asking starts at home. They must manage the asking of children and husbands, from first call in the morning to last call at night. After mothers come children. What is the first thing on a newborn baby's 'to-do list'? Ask! Crying is asking for food, for attention, for love. Babies grow into children, but the asking never stops. How mothers manage their little askers make lifetime differences in families. It's called parenting. Sure, fathers are also on stage, but they are often bit players. Mothers play the lead role."

We were enjoying an unhurried dinner with our wives, sitting at a cozy table in front of a glowing fire in a 60-year-old restaurant built of logs. A perfect setting for thoughtful conversation. We ordered dessert and coffee. Our wives participated in the exchange of insights. The conversation flowed.

"Asking is tiered. While it starts with families, asking tiers extend to the highest positions of leadership. Presidents, business CEOs, teachers, coaches, pastors, priests, rabbis, professionals, fundraisers. Leaders must manage tiers of askers."

"Leaders are the premier askers, and if they're good leaders, they share their vision with the people they lead so everyone works toward the same goal and shares in the rewards."

"Premier askers receive the greatest rewards because they receive benefits from the askers they manage."

"Right, and the rewards can be tangible, like profits, increased sales, or simply more hugs, or they can be intangible, like freedom and intergenerational sustainability."

"The premier askers control the most important choices in families, the workplace, communities, and even in nations and global affairs."

"Politicians and their staffs set goals to raise millions of dollars from contributors to be elected to public office. Candidates must create a vision for the tiers of workers who will ask donors for money. The vision must include rewards for all those engaged in the process."

Business successes and failures can be predicted by evaluating the efficiency of the way asking—and askers—are managed. The boss is The One, the person in charge of the askers. Employees are both askers and receivers. Customers are also askers and receivers.

In the restaurant where we were dining, for example, the boss's performance would be evaluated by how many customers, especially repeat customers, his or her employees serve. The employees would be evaluated according to customer satisfaction, indicated by compliments, smiles, tips, and performance ratings. The benefit for the customer is, of course, a good meal at a fair price, courteously and efficiently served. How good, how fair, how courteous, and how efficient depend on how the boss manages the employees.

Profitable, growing businesses always hire good askers at each tier of responsibility.

Organization Effectiveness

Our dinner party became a spirited conversation as we realized the importance of managing askers. We wondered if we had stumbled upon another piece of the "effective asking" puzzle. Can "asker management" be taught? Is it a new way of evaluating leadership? Academically, does it fall within the purview of psychology, communications, political science, business? Perhaps it is all those and more.

FIVE-STAR ASKERS

If you Google "five star," you will find over 116 million results. That's a lot of stars—enough to justify labeling the "five star" phrase as a cliché.

There is a reason it is so overused: It signifies the best we can hope to be or experience. The ranks of five-star general and admiral are the highest currently awarded in the military. Five-star hotels claim to be the best luxury hotels in the world. Five-star banks advertise they provide the best service to customers. Five-star pet grooming connects owners and their four-legged friends with quality pet care. Readers rate books with stars. We all need points of reference for our expectations.

In conversations, I often found myself referring to good askers as five-star askers. I began to measure myself and others by my own arbitrary five-star scale. Don't we all want to do something first-rate and top-notch? Five-star askers are the most effective people on a scale of 1 to 5 because they ask most effectively. They get what they want. They are Master Askers.

Ron's Confidence Changes

Ron, a client and friend from high school, failed at most things he tried in life until he learned how to ask effectively. Ron's father was an alcoholic, working as a machinist in a factory by day and in front of the television with a glass of vodka in his hand every evening. His mother was submissive. Their small house was in desperate need of cleaning and maintenance. Ron's parents had no expectations for him beyond repeating their own mistakes.

He began fulfilling those low expectations early on. He failed the third grade. He had no self-confidence, no self-esteem. In high school, he did not take college preparatory classes because no one expected him to go to college. He was always on the football team's third-string, even though he was a fast runner, because he did not expect to excel—and didn't. In tackling practice, he always ended up being our human tackling dummy, standing in the tackling pit waiting to be hit by the next runner. The love of his life in high school gave her affections away to everyone but Ron.

When Ron and I worked summer jobs together, we always ended up doing the dirtiest work: digging ditches, filling cracks in the street with tar, hauling cement, and climbing up the highest trees to trim the branches by hand. I was learning what I did not want to do in life. Ron seemed resigned to the next dirty job. He was a wonderful friend—agreeable, reliable, humorous, and in possession of an old car that we all used for transportation around town—but Ron did not know how to change his path.

He actually did try college. We roomed together one semester. On weekend nights, I could hear him quietly sobbing in bed, his grade point average plummeting, his social life a disaster, and his money running low. He dropped out.

Finally, at age 21, with encouragement from friends, he took control of his life and began to ask effectively for help. First, he returned to school. He applied for admission to Colorado College, a small private liberal arts college in Colorado Springs. He begged to be accepted, and he was, but on probation, conditional on succeeding in summer school classes. Succeed he did, literally studying day and night.

Ron attended class during the day, then worked as a night watchman at a pharmaceutical laboratory. As the night-shift security guard, he was paid to sit behind a desk doing nothing—except study. He became fascinated with the research going on in the laboratory by scientists developing new drugs to treat high blood pressure.

Professors began to take an interest in him when his grades rose consistently to A's and B's. He began to ask very provocative questions in class. His laboratory work always included extra-credit assignments. His contagious smile and laughter lifted everyone's spirits, in and out of class. He received a partial scholarship based on academic improvement after one year.

Nearing graduation, he decided to continue his studies and earned a Ph.D. in biochemistry, with an emphasis on pharmacology, the science of medical drugs. Although he received rejections from several graduate schools, Ron continued to ask effectively for admission until he was accepted at the University of Manitoba in Canada. There, he successfully completed his studies to earn a Ph.D. and began to help research new drugs. His Canadian lab assistant became his sweetheart, his wife, and the mother of his son.

Upon graduation, Ron was hired by Eli Lilly and Company to join a research team investigating heart medications. He became their lead research scientist in developing new medicines to limit heart damage during a heart attack and led the way in developing a treatment breakthrough. His fame began to spread throughout the industry. He was hired away from Eli Lilly by a small start-up biotech that offered him a top technical position and a share of ownership in the company. His self-esteem and productivity soared. The new company prospered. An initial public offering (IPO) made Ron a multimillionaire. He began traveling the world, explaining research techniques, new experimental medical drugs, and visions of future pharmaceuticals.

As a lifelong friend, I watched Ron's performance change from no stars to five stars. First, he convinced himself he was capable of achievement. Then, he began to ask effectively for help, again and again, until he achieved his goals. You can become a five-star asker. First know what you want. Then, ask effectively for it—persistently.

Ron, in fact, eventually crashed from his five-star life. Instead of working from a concern for other people and a passion for science, he became obsessed with protecting and increasing his financial wealth. He began to see the government as his enemy because of the taxes he paid on his income. He stopped reaching out to ask for help, or to offer help.

At one point, Ron decided to build an experimental aircraft. He knew nothing about flying, but he diligently studied to obtain a pilot's license and passed the test with high scores. He hired an aircraft mechanic to help build the experimental aircraft. He was fascinated by the freedom he felt in the air at the controls of his own single-engine plane. I accepted his offer to fly together, but the time and location never seemed to fit for both of us.

Tragically, when Ron took the experimental aircraft for a test flight, at an altitude of about 500 feet above ground, the motor began to sputter. Ron panicked. Although he had earned his license, he had nowhere near the experience he needed to pilot a plane of untested design, and he was so expectant of his own successes by now that he hadn't asked for guidance or help. Instead of flying straight and pancaking it into an adjacent field, he turned, tilting the aircraft to the right. It lost altitude immediately, stalled, and cartwheeled to the ground. After impact, Ron never regained consciousness.

Is there any risk to becoming a five-star asker? Yes. The risk is over-confidence, believing you're always destined to succeed because you're somehow entitled to. Experience shows that five-star askers often fall from their pedestals because they begin to ignore or forget to apply the 5 Win Words. They stop asking for help.

THE WIN-WIN OUTCOME

Big R called on a Saturday morning. That was unusual for a guy who regularly fills his weekends with family activities. Asking was on his mind.

"The giver is also an asker!" he blurted.

"What do you mean?" I asked him.

"Both have expectations. Both have wants. Each must take away something. One may get a bigger return."

"Satisfaction?"

"Yes, there has to be a satisfaction to the giver," he observed, "either instantly or along the way. It's not a one-way street. Rewards must flow in both directions. There should be a win-win outcome. The giver will not participate unless he receives a return benefit—love, friendship, gratitude, recognition, opportunity, helping humanity, warm smile—something."

"Give me a simple example," I urged.

"Buying a prospective client or customer breakfast," he quickly responded. "The person's immediate want is satisfied. Food! He may decide to use your service or buy your product as a result of the breakfast meeting. You receive a benefit. A meaningful personal relationship may evolve. To enjoy a positive outcome, both your expectations must be satisfied."

I thought back to the early years when I was struggling to build a private law practice. Big R was riding the financial roller-coaster as a real estate sales person. We were both trying to support growing families. Occasionally, I invited him and his wife to our home for an informal dinner. Spontaneous ideas to help each other's careers were part of the chatter at the table. Predictably, in the following months, he would direct some law work my way.

"I give to my church because I hope there will be a reward in heaven," Big R continued. "Maybe it will help me get there. I give to charities to help less fortunate people. Free meals. Clothing. Vaccinations. Books. Computers. Goods and services for the poor. Bill Gates gives to help mankind. Let's be honest, we also give because we get a tax deduction, more money in our pockets. Charitable givers have expectations. They receive many satisfactions for their donations."

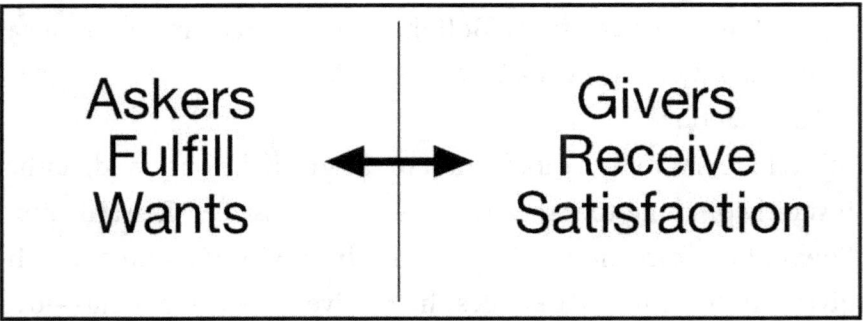

Rita Built Confidence

A client named Rita recounts a relevant story. She started a nonprofit organization to give scholarships to underprivileged first-generation college aspirants. Her bank account contained only enthusiasm and commitment, and she was unsure of her fundraising abilities. She decided to challenge herself before challenging others. She explained at a luncheon I attended how she built the self-confidence needed for her project.

> I wanted to attend an educational conference in Miami. The conference was focused on expanding educational opportunities for underprivileged college students. There was no way I could afford the conference fee, airline ticket, or expense. The first thing I did was call the conference coordinator in Miami, explained why I needed to attend, and asked if they would give me a complementary admission to the conference. When I explained what I was doing, she agreed to give me free entry, then added, "We need more people like you." Next, I needed transportation. I called an airline. The woman who answered happened to be the secretary to a vice-president, so I told her what I needed. She put me through directly to the vice-president. I talked fast, stating that I had just talked to the conference co-coordinator in Miami. She had given me a free ticket to the conference, but I had no way of getting there. Would he please donate a round-trip ticket? "Of course," he said, just like that! Then he startled me by adding, "Thank you for asking. These opportunities to help deserving folks like you don't come along very often."
> Next, I called a hotel close to the conference. I asked for the general manager. When she came on the line, I explained I had a complimentary pass to the conference and free airline pass. I wondered if there might be some way she could help with lodging for three days. She asked several questions about the conference, then offered, "Yes, we can do that. We all need to help educate our young people. Please give me your name and e-mail for the confirmation."

I guess you can get anything you want if you keep your expectations high, ask for what you want, and try to satisfy everyone's wants.

By asking effectively, Rita created her own opportunity. Unknowingly, perhaps instinctively, her actions reflected the philosophy of one of the great, historic leaders of the free world, who was a premier asker.

> I like things to happen;
> And if they don't happen,
> I like to make them happen.
> —Winston Churchill

Take the lead in your own life. Make things happen. Ask effectively for what you want. Keep your expectations high. Try to satisfy the needs and desires of everyone involved. Positive outcomes will flow abundantly.

APPENDIX

APPENDIX

YOUR *ASK EFFECTIVELY* ACTION PLAN

Do you have an ASK Effectively action plan? Will your questions be simple, direct, and focused? Have you thought through the Ws of planning: What? Who? Why? When? Where?

Ask yourself before asking others. If you have answers to the five W questions, you have a thoughtful action plan with a high probability of getting the results you want.

If possible, take time for reflection. Avoid emotion-packed questions. Use this fast and easy form to focus your ASK Effectively action plan.

ASK Effectively Action Plan

1. What to ask:
2. Who to ask:
3. Why ask:
4. When to ask:
5. Where to ask:

Date:_____

Repeat to improve. Develop an ASK Effectively action plan for each important question you pose to someone. Keep a record of results. The outcomes will improve over time as you learn how to ask effectively.

ASK Effectively Action Plan

1. What to ask:
2. Who to ask:
3. Why ask:
4. When to ask:
5. Where to ask:

Date:_____

Repeat to expand your asking by adding new questions seeking help.

YOUR *ASK EFFECTIVELY* RATING

Do you ask effectively? How can you improve personal outcomes? Use this fast and easy self-evaluation form to rate your performance in applying the 5 Win Words. Rate your performance for each Win Word with a score of 1 to 20. Add scores to determine your ASK Effectively rating.

Ask Effectively Rating

WIN WORDS	PERFORMANCE RATING 1= lowest, 20 = highest
1. Persistence	Score:
2. Sincerity	Score:
3. Humility	Score:
4. Honesty	Score:
5. Belief	Score:
Overall rating (maximum 100):	

Date:_____

Invite others to rate themselves. Even consider rating each other. Share and discuss results, including how to improve actual performance.

Ask Effectively Rating

WIN WORDS	PERFORMANCE RATING 1= lowest, 20 = highest
1. Persistence	Score:
2. Sincerity	Score:
3. Humility	Score:
4. Honesty	Score:
5. Belief	Score:
Overall rating (maximum 100):	

Date:_____

Repeat occasionally to track changes. Keep and record your ratings. Expect better results as your ASK Effectively rating increases.

HUMBLE THANKS

To Big R, who prefers anonymity.

To my inspirational intergenerational family, Dorothy, Christina, Leonard, Ericka, Eric, Tyler, Tammy, Zachary, Sarah, Hannah, Charles, Adam, Sandy, Kai and Cary, limitless gratitude for showing me new ways to ask.

To Cydney Campbell, J.D., for her spirited support in endlessly organizing and editing iterations of the manuscript with a smile; Gregory Daries, for his usual graphics brilliance; Gene Brissie, a beacon of light on the stormy seas of book publishing; Ernie Trembly, a master at making a manuscript reader-friendly; Toni Knapp, editor extraordinaire; Lonny Elliott, an insightful salesman and more; R II, a loyal follower of Big R; and Kirk Woundy, whose journalistic talents were highly appreciated in the third and fourth editions.

To clients, friends, medical patients and providers, and others, for the unreported stories, the stories behind the personal headlines, the stories that illustrate the power of asking. Personal identities and related information have been changed to preserve confidentiality and privacy, unless permission was granted.

Credit has been given, and sources of information cited, where appropriate. If additional credit is due, please excuse and contact me to assure inclusion in the next edition. Writing a book always includes asking for help from many players.

To Donald Kallaus, Rhyolite Press LLC for an extraordinary professional commitment in designing the Fourth Edition in record time.

www.ingramcontent.com/pod-product-compliance
Lightning Source LLC
LaVergne TN
LVHW020928090426
835512LV00020B/3261